Excerpts from Letters

An amazing story, and when I read it to the survivors at our Board of Directors they were touched. . . . Thank you very much for the opportunity to read it to those still alive.

Marie-Claire du Bois, daughter of a political prisoner who died at Ellrich, Secretary of the Belgian Association of Survivors of Dora

It is with much emotion and great feeling of recognition that I received your book so well written and so well documented. . . . In a few more days I would have died. John Galione and his fellow soldiers saved my life!

Michel Depierre, Dora Survivor

I received and read your manuscript. My God, what a book! The story of your family is enthralling. . . .

Yves Beon, Dora Survivor

It is an amazing story about a remarkable man. . . . We will always be grateful to your father and the amazing story you recorded for him. Thank you on behalf of all our family for writing down what happened . . . to think of all the lives he saved. Not only the prisoners, but all their descendants!

Charles Lang, Nordhausen Survivor, and his wife, Joan

You told it exactly the way it was . . . I thank your father times 57 years!

George Benedict, Dora Survivor

Just finished reading the book. Could not put it down. Your father's story is amazing. . . . a book I heartily recommend.

M. G., Dora-Nordhausen Sub-Camp Liberator, 104th ID

I started reading the book and could not put it down. Maybe all those missiles that the U.S. got from Germany would be in Russian hands. John Galione made the big difference! Everyone should read this book!

D. M., Dora-Nordhausen liberator, 104th ID

I have just finished reading your EXCELLENT book. I cried numerous times while reading. . . . You are to be congratulated for the excellent research you have done in documenting this WWII story. You can be sure that I will be recommending this book to all of my friends. . . . I am so happy that your dad's story is out there for all to see and reflect upon. And what a story it is!! All Timberwolves should read this book. . . . I am SO everlasting grateful to you for writing this book, Mary. You have helped clear up the mysteries in this chapter of my life.

R. R., Eye-Witness to Nordhausen atrocities, 329th Engineers

WOW! What a story. There are many things that touched me. You write so that one gets a sense of anticipation and you don't want to lay down the book.

L. T., Dora-Nordhausen Liberator, 555th FAB

A true life story which moved my heart and soul. God bless your dad. . . . His story must be told to generations.

J. M. P., Alaska

How can I ever thank you for the privilege of reading your excellent and moving book. It is a truly amazing story that had me in its grip as I read from cover to cover in 24 hours.

N. Y., UK

Read this book! You'll never be the same.

P., Book Reviewer

I am a lover of history. This book is packed full of it. I learned things I never knew had happened. I recommend this book to those who love history and want more knowledge about World War II and the holocaust.

E., Book Reviewer

Anyone within earshot has been hearing me rave about your book. . . . I feel like I just completed an enthralling history class, which held my attention the whole way through. I kept wishing I was a faster reader, as I couldn't turn the pages fast enough!

T. N., Publishing Consultant

I finished reading your book. . . . Your report kept me amazed: the details of the rockets, the details of Nazi Germany, and the details of those poor, poor people that were emaciated and starved. It swept me off my feet and I am so glad I read it. People need to read this book.

J. O., The Netherlands

An excellent book and I found it moving and educational.

Jamie

This should be a movie. The story of an Italian boy raised during the depression is interesting enough, but this is a story that should be read by young and old alike, about WWII and the horror of the holocaust. . . . A must read in a day when some say this never happened. Ms. Nahas did her homework on the ballistic missile developed by German scientists. I highly recommend this book.

D. S., Book Reviewer

Words can never express what I am experiencing because of the time you have taken to honor your father. . . . What an amazing story. Thank you so much for coming to our school. I will carry the sound of our students' applause at your father's words with me to my grave.

D. A., Teacher

I just read your father's story of finding Dora. I am touched by his humility and strength. To have the ability to listen to the inner voice of God during war is truly remarkable.

C. C.

What I hear a lot in daily life is we need heroes for the kids to admire and we don't have them. How wrong they are. We do have heroes and your dad and the men from the 104th Timberwolf have to be called heroes; a gift from God.

M. G., Military Organization

I just stood there hugging the book, and crying.

J. S.

THE HEROIC JOURNEY

OF

PRIVATE GALIONE

The Holocaust Liberator Who Changed History

MARY NAHAS

The Heroic Journey of Private Galione: The Holocaust Liberator Who Changed History
© 2012 by Mary Galione-Nahas All Rights Reserved Worldwide
Second Edition - Revised and Updated
The Journey of Private Galione: How America Became A Superpower © 2004

No part of this publication may be reproduced, stored in a retrieval system, scanned, transmitted, or distributed in any way by any means—electronic, mechanical, photocopy, recording or otherwise—without the prior written permission from the copyright holder.

ISBN 10: 0615700039
ISBN-13: 978-0615700038

In memory of the victims of Mittelbau Dora and associated concentration camps whose suffering burned in my father's heart. May his message bring hope, healing, and peace.

Contents

	Dedication	vii
	Foreword I	x
	Foreword II	xi
Affidavit from Dora Survivor Organization		xii
Affidavit from Sergeant Leonard Puryear		xiii
	Preface	xv
1	The Making of The Liberator	1
2	The Corresponding Rise of the Rocket and the Reich	17
3	The Nightmare of Camp Dora and War	33
4	Saving the Prisoners of Dora	53
5	The American Capture of Missile Technology	81
6	Decoding History: God and the Holocaust	97
7	A Message Emerged	105
	Photos	111
	Acknowledgements	117
	Bibliography	118
	End Notes to Chapter 4	120
	Memorial	122

Foreword I

Being a survivor of the Dora Concentration Camp, I was much honored when Mary asked me to write a foreword to this book. I was not in Hell, but I believe that the concentration camps of Mittelbau Dora were the closest thing to Hell. After being in Auschwitz, I never thought anything could be as bad as it was there; the only difference was that there were no gas chambers at Dora. Daily people died by the dozens. At Dora there were people from all over Europe: Greeks, Italians, Poles, Yugoslavs, Dutch, Czechs, Jews, French, and Russians—even Germans.

Some of the well-known persons who were in charge of the German rocket production witnessed the inhuman treatment of the prisoners. These same people were later brought to the United States and placed in charge of our missile production (Wernher von Braun, Arthur Rudolph, and many others).

Private John Michael Galione of the 104th "Timberwolf" Army Infantry Division was a modern-day Moses on that April day in 1945. He not only discovered the concentration camps of Dora and the rocket factories there; he brought us liberation from slavery. Had he come a day later, many more people would have died.

For all the prisoners who survived, I want to thank him. It was God's will that Private Galione found us and we were liberated from the hell of Dora, to bear witness to what happened not only at Dora, but also in all German concentration camps. Today, there are not many of the brave soldiers left who liberated us. To all of you who were there, I want to say "THANK YOU!" I also want to thank Mary Nahas for taking the time and effort to write this wonderful, historical book.

Survivor of Mittelbau Dora Concentration Camp, George B. Benedict
California, 2004

Foreword II

I am a survivor of Nordhausen Death Camp. Because Private John Galione did not give up on following the railroad tracks and finding the gates of Camp Dora, I am alive today. Because Private Galione notified the other members of the 104th Infantry Division, the German camps began to be liberated on April 11, 1945. Ironically, I was found and rescued on my 16th birthday, April 15, 1945, when I was near death.

If only I could have thanked John Galione for his perseverance and bravery, which saved my life and the lives of others. However, I have been fortunate enough to meet his daughter Mary Galione-Nahas and her family, to whom I can express my deep and everlasting gratitude. Mary did a great service to both her father's memory and all of the victims of Nazism by chronicling her father's determination to "follow the tracks."

Today, I am a grateful American citizen, happily married, with three children and seven grandchildren.

Survivor of Nordhausen Death Camp, Charles Lang
July 25, 2012

AMICALE		VRIENDENKRING
DES	DORA	DER
PRISONNIERS POLITIQUES	B	**POLITIEKE GEVANGENEN**
DE		VAN
DORA ET COMMANDOS		DORA EN KOMMANDOS
A.S.B.L.		V.Z.W.D.
Siège Social :		Maatschappelijke Zetel
C.N.P.P.A.		N.C.P.G.R.
Rue du Commerce, 21	Compte 210-0970034-86 Rekening	Handelsstraat, 21
1000 BRUXELLES		1000 BRUSSEL

courrier et contacts: C/O Marie-Claire du Bois de Vroylande, secrétaire
Rue de Mollendael, 2 B-1320 Beauvechain Belgique tel & fax 00 32 10 86 67 69

Témoignage de John M. Galione
avril 1945

Découverte des camps de concentration de DORA et de NORDHAUSEN

décembre 2000

**Affidavit from the Mittelbau Dora Survivor Organization
in Belgium confirming Galione's discovery.**

August 15, 2000

While on a scouting mission, Pfc. John M. Galione, serial number 33812812, was the first American soldier to discover Mittelbau Dora Concentration Camp in Nordhausen, Germany. Private Galione returned to his platoon to report his discovery on April 11, 1945, and the liberation of the prisoners of Camp Dora was then organized. Private Galione was a member of the 104th Timberwolf Army Infantry Division, 415th regiment, company B.

Leonard T. Puryear   8-21-00
Signature   Date

T, SGT
Rank during April 11, 1945

104 Th Timberwolf Army Infantry Division
Army Infantry Division and regiment   _Co.B - 415th Regiment_

Judith P. Stallings   8-21-00
Signature of Notary   Date

My Commission expires
3-17-2005

**Affidavit from Galione's WWII Sergeant,
Leonard Puryear, confirming his discovery.**

Preface

Before I was born Dad never talked much about his childhood or the war; he kept his grief to himself. But, God in His wisdom joined us with a bond that caused my father to take me under his wing as though I were an apprentice. From the time I was able to listen and understand he began shaping my character with stories of his childhood and the war. With love, I made it my life's quest to listen and help him find peace. Through the years I sat patiently, gently swaying him to open up the deepest chambers of his heart.

"Tell me about your life, Daddy. What was it like growing up on the farm? What did you go through in the war?" I never dreamed becoming his closest confidant would cause him to reveal a war story he had kept secret for fifty years, a story he would have otherwise taken to his grave.

During World War II, Mittelbau Dora Concentration Camp housed the most top-secret factory in Germany. Deep in a labyrinth of dark, underground caves running through the Harz Mountains, emaciated slave laborers from Buchenwald and other camps worked under the lash of brutal Nazi guards, struggling to manufacture the world's first ballistic missile—a highly advanced weapon for which the world had no defense. Those too weak to work were dumped and left to die in a Dora sub-camp called, Boelcke Kaserne, commonly referred to as, Nordhausen Death Camp.

After the liberation of the Dora-Nordhausen complex, rumors circulated amongst the liberators of the 104th "Timberwolf" Army Infantry Division that the camp had actually been discovered by a lone Timberwolf soldier. After the war, one of the veterans appeared on National television, urging the veteran who discovered the complex to come forward and be recognized for his discovery. Dora survivors had actually seen the lone soldier trying to break into the camp two days before liberating troops arrived at Dora, one day before they arrived at Nordhausen. According to Sophie Samuels, daughter of Dora survivor Michel Depierre, the survivors attended Timberwolf reunions after the war in an effort to find that

The Heroic Journey of Private Galione

soldier. "They wanted to thank him for saving them," she said "and they wanted to know the story of how he had found them in such a hidden camp where the work was so secret."

What they didn't know is that the Timberwolf soldier they searched for who had discovered Camp Dora was my father, Private John Michael Galione of the 104th Army Infantry Division, but his story had been silenced on April 11, 1945. Moreover, the story they longed to hear held the answers to their most important questions, such as: "If God loved us so much, then why didn't He save us before the evacuation of the camps? Did He at least care about our suffering? Why were our perpetrators rewarded rather than punished for their crimes?"

My father kept his story to himself for over 50 years, but after a lifetime of mulling over the events, a deeper and more significant story emerged that my father realized would mean a lot to those who suffered in the camps and to those who lost loved ones. "Tell them my story, Mary," he said. "When you tell them the story, don't just tell them how I found them, but tell them about what happened to me before and after the war."

Therefore, my father's story doesn't begin with the war; it begins with the enthralling story of his childhood. Finally, after seven years of writing and researching, the survivors can know the miracle of how they were found and rescued, they can learn of the meaningful holocaust memorial that emerged from my father's life, and the world can discover how one soldier's faith, courage, and persistence saved thousands in the camps and changed world history.

July 25, 2012, Mary Galione-Nahas

Chapter 1

The Making of The Liberator

The morning sun peeked over the hill. A rooster's crow pierced the silence. Inside a Long Island farmhouse Elisabetta wiped the sleep from her eyes and pulled her gray hair back in a bun. She dragged her feet to the kitchen and cooked breakfast in her favorite black-iron pan. Bread dough made the night before flopped over the brim of a large bowl. Thoughts of a hearty meal lured little Johnny in from milking the cows. With excitement he plopped a heavy bucket of fresh warm milk down onto the wood-plank floor. "Time to punch down the dough," Elisabetta shouted to her children in Italian. "Then later we'll have fresh bread!"

Johnny enjoyed life on the farm, but much of his childhood was spent working terribly hard for his mother and father, Elisabetta and Raffael. They were from a different era in time. Born in the late 1870s, they were raised hard by stern fathers in the small farming village of Casaluce, located 20 km north of Naples, Italy. In those days survival was tough. Men ruled their wives and children with an iron hand, and they made them work as hard as men. Women and children who failed to share the workload faced the wrath of the *capo di casa* (Italian for "Head of the House").

In the early 1900s, Elisabetta and Raffael left Naples with their children and boarded a ship headed for America. They passed through Ellis Island, hoping to benefit from the so-called streets of gold. Securing their roots, they rented a dilapidated farmhouse resting on a beautiful farm in the rural village of Wyandanch, unaware that gold had been buried on the farm years earlier only a few feet from the front porch!

Back then life revolved around the farm. Elisabetta had never known what it felt like to go shopping or to see a movie. She never left the farm. Her days were spent planting, harvesting, preserving food, cooking, making soap from lye, washing clothes on a washboard, working like a horse, and having babies. Some of her babies were born in the field as she farmed. She'd walk back to the house, wrap the baby in a blanket, and go back to work in the field.

Johnny was born in the Long Island farmhouse on January 25, 1919. He was the eighth child of eleven children: Marcellino, Annie, Josephine, Frankie, Jimmy, Nicky, the first Johnny, the second Johnny, twin girls, and Mary, who was later born on a Pennsylvania farm. Besides several miscarriages, Elisabetta lost Josephine (in her mid-twenties) to spinal meningitis, twin baby girls, and the "first" Johnny died at the age of five while Elisabetta was pregnant with the "second" Johnny: Johnny tells the story:

> My mother never got over my brother's death. My name was supposed to be Paul, but my mother loved Johnny so much she gave me his name. The strongest memory I have of my mother is her sitting in a rocking chair, crying. It made me feel so sad to see my mother cry like that. I'd jump on her lap to cheer her up and she'd hug and kiss me all over my face. Oh, she was such an affectionate woman. She loved us all so much. She was probably crying over *all* the children she had lost.
>
> We had it hard, but some immigrants had it worse. We were lucky we had the farm. Many Italians who came to this country couldn't find jobs, and they had no way to get food because they didn't have the farm to turn to. They had to starve. My father, Raffael, helped a family that was starving. There was a man from Naples who was originally from Sicily. He had come to America and settled in Long Island. He had a family to feed and had been trying to find work for months. That's how it was back then. In those days, Italians were treated with prejudice. Nobody would hire us because we were Italian. If they did hire us, they gave us the dirty backbreaking jobs that paid very little. The man and his family were starving. He became desperate and agreed to do something small for the Mafia for money in order to feed his family. But after he did that, they wanted him to do something else—*something big*—and he refused.

You see, you just can't say *no* to the Mafia when they want you to do something. Especially after they've taken you in and introduced you to everybody, and you learn what everybody's doing. This man's whole family was in *serious* danger of being killed. My father felt sorry for them. He knew how hard it was to come from another country and survive in America, and he felt a kinship toward them because they were from Naples. So, he let the family move in with us in exchange for help on the farm. He figured there were so many of us kids always running around on the farm that no one would know the difference if we added a few more to the bunch. Our neighbors weren't that close to our house. They didn't really know who we all were. All they knew is that they could see from a distance a bunch of people of all ages always outside farming.

Even though there were so many of us kids, my father didn't mind the family moving in. In fact, he liked having them because they were a big help on the farm. We always had so much work to do. They had a young boy about twelve or thirteen who helped a great deal with our workload. He made it easier for me too. I didn't have as many chores to do, and it enabled me to have a little fun.

Raffael warned Johnny never to tell anyone the family had moved in or they could all be killed. Johnny was instructed to tell others that the people living there were *fratello* and *sorella* (Italian for "brother and sister"). They were "Galiones." Although he was a young boy, Johnny understood and obeyed his father. Over time the family moved away, but to insure their safety they continued using the Galione surname. Today, the decedents of the family Raffael harbored almost eighty years ago live on. This experience taught Johnny the value of risking his life to save others.

A CRY OF ECHOES IN THE DARK

Aside from strangers moving in to hide from the Mafia, there were stranger and more frightening things going on in the New York farmhouse after dark. Galione explains:

The Heroic Journey of Private Galione

When we'd go to bed at night we'd hear drumbeats, chanting, screaming, and the sound of running feet. In the middle of the night my brother, my sisters and I used to meet in the hall outside our bedroom. We'd sit and huddle together, afraid, and try to figure out what those noises could be. You see, down from the steps of the front porch was a big oak tree. By the oak tree there was a slab of rock of some sort and it looked like it was covering something. Sometimes, as I ran back and forth doing chores on the farm, I'd get an eerie feeling when I'd pass by the rock. Something was drawing me to go over there and look underneath. We had a hunch that the sounds we heard at night had something to do with whatever was under that rock. My father believed something was under there. Every night he had the same dream: that if we dug up the rock we would become wealthy. He always wanted to dig it up, but he never had the time. He was always working until very late at night.

Meanwhile, Douglas Fairbanks and his film crew passed by the Galione farm and found themselves captivated by the breathtaking view of the mountain behind the house. Within days the owner of the farm told Raffael that Fairbanks had bought the farm, so Raffael and his family had to move. When Fairbanks and his associates saw the massive stone near the front porch, a gut feeling compelled them to dig it up and look underneath.

The stone stood seven feet long, four feet wide, and stuck out of the ground six to eight inches. With old-fashioned picks and shovels of the early 1920s, it took hours for Fairbanks' crew to bust through the thick slab. When the rock finally gave way they were astounded by what they saw inside. The crew had unearthed the burial ground of a massacred tribe of Native Americans, and lying in the bottom of the pit was the faded picture of their Chief framed in solid gold! This experience taught Johnny that people can sometimes hear the cries of blood that was shed in innocence.

THE RIVER INCIDENT

Once the grave was uncovered the noises and strange occurrences stopped. As Fairbanks planned to knock down the old house and build a new one, the Galione family moved to Starkey's Farm in Pennsylvania. As Raffael prospered, he purchased a 500-acre tract of land located on the adjoining King's Farm. The house sat alongside Van Sciver Lake near the Delaware River in Tullytown's rural Wheat Sheaf village. King's Farm was beautiful country, but living near the Delaware River posed a serious danger in the winter months. During the bitter-cold winters, when temperatures would plummet to around zero, the river froze solid and local children went skating. Galione recalls that day:

> One morning there were no chores to do because the fields were covered in snow. After feeding the chickens there was little else for me to do, so I walked down to the river to see if the neighborhood kids were skating. We didn't have ice skates in those days. We had fun sliding on the ice in our shoes. When I reached the river I was disappointed. Not a soul was in sight. It was so cold that day that everybody stayed inside to keep warm by their fireplaces and coal stoves.
>
> I knew better than to step out onto the ice alone, but the voice of temptation kept saying, "Go ahead. Skate all the way out to the middle. It will be fun!" I stepped out onto the ice and skated out to almost the middle of the river. I was having fun sliding around in my shoes when all of a sudden a soft spot gave way and I fell through the ice.
>
> My only way out from under the ice was through the hole that my body made when I fell through the ice, but the current carried me away from it. The water was *freezing cold!* It was a struggle, but I thought I had managed to swim against the current back to where I had fallen in. I swam around looking for the hole, but it was dark under the ice.

I was swimming around for quite a while trying to find my way out. There was nothing but a solid wall of ice over me. I started to panic because I had held my breath for quite a while and I needed to breathe. I needed air. I remember thinking, "I'm going to die and my family will never know what happened to me. They'll never find me. I'll either be trapped under the ice until it thaws in the spring, or the current will wash my body out to the ocean where sharks and fish will eat me. My mother still cries for all of her children who died. If I die here under the ice, she won't even know where my body is. It will kill her. My poor mother."

That was the last thing I remember thinking *under* the water when I found myself laying on the ground *beside* the water. For the life of me, I don't know how I got out of the water and onto the banks of the river! I tried to remember finding the hole and climbing across the ice onto the ground, but I had no recollection of it. I looked all around trying to find who might have rescued me, but there was no one in sight for miles and I could see far because there was nothing but farmland and everything was all white, covered in snow.

I looked to see if someone had left footprints so I could follow them and thank who rescued me, but there was only one set of footprints in the snow and they were mine. I could see the hole I fell through. It was still only as wide as my torso. I thought, "Surely if someone had crossed the ice in a boat to pull me out they would have had to break the ice as they move across the river to the hole, and they would have had to break the ice around the hole where I fell through in order to pull me out." But there was no additional broken ice. Everything was exactly the way it was when I fell in.

I couldn't stay there looking any longer. I was soaking wet and *freezing* cold. Colder than you can ever imagine! I was so cold I was stiff. I could hardly move my arms and legs, but I made myself get up and walk, and it was quite a ways to get back home. It was hard to move, but I knew if I stayed there I would freeze to death right there on the ground next to the river.

I thought when I got home I would be in big trouble for what I had done. In an Italian family you get hit for causing yourself harm or making your parents worry. That's how they teach you common sense. But when I walked into the kitchen frozen with ice hanging off me and shaking like a leaf, and when my mother looked at me and saw that I had almost drowned under the ice, and when she realized that she had almost lost another child after losing so many, she became *extremely* emotional.

She grabbed me *hard* and pulled me into her. She was holding me tight, crying out my name, *"Johnny! Johnny!"* and kissing me all over, thanking God over and over again for bringing me back to her. My mother had lost so many children that she couldn't bear the thought of losing one more. She was so grateful that I didn't die, that I came back to her.

After the river incident, I tried to soothe the pain of my mother's grief. I had to watch my baby sister, Mary, out in the fields while my mother tended crops. I had so much fun playing games with Mary. I used to chase her and she would laugh. She was so cute. My mother would get a kick out of hearing us laugh and play in the fields. When I saw that it made her happy I would do it more. I liked making my mother happy because she had experienced so much hardship in her life that made her sad. It made me feel good to see her laugh.

Sometimes, I'd go to the lake with my mother; we'd sit on a rock and wash clothes together. We used a washboard and the soap she made from lye. I enjoyed helping my mother. I felt sorry for her because she always had too much work to do. She never had time for herself, not even to fix her hair. I enjoyed spending time alone with her by the lake, just me and my mother.

John Galione at 12-years-old standing by his home on Logan Street in Bristol, PA.

HARDSHIP AND CHARACTER

While Elisabetta taught Johnny love and affection, Raffael taught him the raw skills of survival. Raffael stood upright, tall and big-boned. When he spoke, he launched a powerful voice from his diaphragm. Those who knew him feared him because of his stature, his voice, his stern personality, and his incredible strength.

> My father used to hoist a full bushel of tomatoes onto each shoulder and walk ten miles into town to sell them to the Bristol markets, and they weren't the regular size bushels. They were huge! I don't know how he did that. When I got a little older, around nine or ten, he took me with him and I helped him carry one of the bushels. They were heavy! I could hardly carry one of them, let alone two. My father must have been as strong as an ox! That was the first time my father praised me. Even though I couldn't carry the second bushel, he still said I had done good to walk all that way carrying tomatoes.

> We never lacked food because we had the farm, but selling tomatoes is how we earned money to buy the things we didn't have. One time, my mother, my father and I were all in the kitchen. It was early in the morning. My mother was helping my father place the bushels of tomatoes onto his shoulders. Meanwhile, I had been playing around on the floor. My father was getting ready to go out the door to start the long walk into town when I accidentally got under his feet. He tripped over me and the tomatoes fell all over the kitchen floor. He beat me for doing that. Because of me, the tomatoes were damaged and he couldn't make money off them at the market. He needed that money badly for something he was going to buy for the family.

Raffael put Johnny to work on the farm at the tender age of five. In fear of Raffael, Johnny did whatever he was told and dared not to complain about being tired or sore. Over time, Johnny learned to ignore pain while working diligently from sunup to sundown. Although he worked terribly hard, he believed hard work built character and was the good part of his childhood. He believed lack of hard work is why children today have gone astray with drugs and suicide.

> It's because they have too much time on their hands; too much time to think and get into trouble. When I was growing up I had so many chores to do that even if I wanted to kill myself there was no time to think about how to do it. There's nothing like growing up on a farm. Every morning I had to milk the cows before sunrise. I'd go out to the barn around four thirty in the morning, while it was still dark. The buckets of milk were so heavy I could hardly carry them into the house. After punching down the dough we'd eat a hearty breakfast. That's one thing about growing up on a farm; we always had plenty of eggs from the chickens, vegetables we farmed, meat from the animals, and homemade bread.

> After baking the bread and eating breakfast, my mother and I worked together ten hours in the fields picking beans. To give you an idea of how many beans I picked, I'd start working right next to my mother. She'd go in one direction and I'd go the other. As the day went by, I'd look up and I could hardly see her she was so far down the field. From where I was standing she was the size of an ant! My mother picked beans like a machine. She was *fast!*

> By the end of the day, I had picked so many beans my fingers would bleed. My hands hurt so badly I used to wrap them in cloth before I'd go to bed at night; that made them feel a little better so I could get to sleep. Then, the next morning I'd have to start the same routine all over again, and I couldn't complain to my father that my hands hurt. When we got hungry we couldn't stop working in the fields to go in the house and eat lunch. We had to eat whatever was growing in the fields. Sometimes we had peppers; sometimes tomatoes or cucumbers. We'd eat whatever we had growing at the time.

The Making of The Liberator

In those days, we never used a watch or a clock. We'd work in the fields all day. When we'd see the sun setting, we'd all start walking toward the house. It was something. We'd all come in from different directions, yet we always happened to meet on the porch at the same time. Then we'd go in and eat supper. That's when we'd eat the bread my mother made each morning. I loved my mother's homemade bread. It was so good and fresh!

We had so many people in our family that we couldn't fit around a regular table. We ate on two big wooden tables pushed together. My mother didn't have time to cook three meals a day for all of us, so she kept a tall pot on the stove and threw whatever meats and vegetables we farmed into the pot. We didn't have indoor plumbing. She'd go outside to pump water from the well into the pot and keep it simmering on low all day. Whenever you got hungry, you just poured yourself a bowl of soup. We ate healthy back then and we were *strong!*

Johnny didn't mind working hard on the farm, but the conditions he had to endure during the Great Depression were painful and hard for him to discuss.

I had to walk miles to school every day in deep snow with no boots on. I imagine I walked about three or four miles to get to school. My feet used to freeze. By the time I got to school I couldn't feel my feet. I had to pick the ice from inside my shoes and from my toes. One time, I had frostbite *real* bad. They were afraid I might lose my toes. Wearing a pair of holey shoes and no socks, I walked from King's Farm in Wheat Sheaf to the schoolhouse in what is now known as the town of Edgely.

There were too many of us. My mother couldn't afford to buy boots for all of us. Sometimes, she'd get a pair and my sister would get them because she was a girl. My sister felt sorry for me and let me take turns wearing them. When I got to school I couldn't speak English. My mother and father spoke only Italian, so I couldn't learn English from them. I had to teach myself. That was the hardest thing I ever had to do when I was growing up.

When we got sick we never went to the doctor. We'd get ear infections so bad we could hardly bear the pain. My mother would pour oil as hot as we could stand into our ears, but we didn't have antibiotics like they give you today. We had to get better on our own. The only time I saw a doctor was when I got blood poisoning. He made me sit outside in a chair and he put a long tube up my leg. He was trying to suck out the poison. The pain was so unbearable, I almost passed out. In fact, I think I did.

My father used to feel sorry for the migrant workers who had families to feed. They couldn't find decent jobs and their children were starving. They would come around asking if there was any work they could do on our farm. Even when he didn't need any help, my father would let them work for big bags of potatoes and other vegetables. He'd even give them wages if he had made out good at the markets and had a little extra left over to share. Sometimes he'd give them big bags of food and let them go their way without having to work. That's how my father was. He would share whatever we had with people who were having a hard time, *especially* if they had small children to feed.

A SIGNIFICANT VOW

Growing up during the Depression brought about an incident that left a mark on Johnny for the rest of his life. Raffael worked like a horse trying to support his family. He farmed and supplied the Bristol markets with fruits and vegetables, he made and sold wine, and he still couldn't meet all the needs of such a large family. The struggle of daily survival caused Raffael to become weary, focused only on the goal of survival. Galione remembers:

> On the farm, we used watchdogs and noisy geese for protection from thieves. There were a lot of thieves in those days because of the Depression. When the dogs began having so many puppies that we couldn't afford to feed them, my father made me bury the puppies, *alive*. I didn't want to do it, but I had to. I was afraid to cross my father. I felt so sorry for those puppies; that they had to die like that. I'd go to bed at night and think about how they had suffered trying to breathe, and how it was me who did that to them. I could hear them whimpering, but I was so afraid my father would find that I didn't get the job done right; I had to stay there and listen until the whimpering stopped. I had to make sure they were dead.

In the first moment of silence anguish overwhelmed Johnny. For weeks he couldn't lay his head upon his pillow at bedtime without hearing the puppies whimper and die all over again. Over time, Johnny understood the circumstances that caused Raffael to make the hasty decision to bury the puppies. He tells the story with sadness:

> My father was so overworked trying to support all of us. Sometimes he wouldn't get back from the markets until midnight, and he had been gone from early in the morning. We didn't have transportation. He walked about ten miles up and ten miles back. By the time he got home he was exhausted. When he got home he couldn't just go to bed; there were more chores for him to do in the barns. Then, he would have to start the same routine all over again early the next morning. That's why he made me bury the puppies: he was tired, and it would be one less responsibility on his shoulders.

Although he understood his father's daily struggle to support a large family, Johnny was a sensitive child with an inborn integrity. He thought about the puppies all his life. As he grew older and developed the ability to reason, Johnny felt ashamed he had buried the puppies out of blind obedience and fear. He realized that if he had mustered up the courage to negotiate, he might have saved the puppies.

"When I look back, there were things I could have done to save the puppies," he explained, "but I was afraid to speak up." In hindsight, as Johnny grew from a boy to a man he stamped in his heart a lesson learned: "I vowed that I would never again out of blind obedience or fear allow an innocent creature to suffer or die senselessly if I had within my power the ability to seek an alternative, no matter the cost to myself." Johnny never dreamed he would face his resolve almost twenty years later during World War II in Germany, when he smelled an ominous odor that he thought might be coming from a concentration camp and was denied permission to begin searching for prisoners.

Having worked hard all his life, Johnny grew strong, skilled, and fearless. He took up boxing at Saint Ann's boxing ring. He dismantled car engines and put them back together. He swam the Delaware River from the Pennsylvania side to New Jersey and back—a two-mile swim in the midst of rolling steamboats—challenging the same currents that had nearly pulled him to his death under the ice years earlier.

Johnny had no idea he was saved from the river so he could grow up to execute a war effort that would save thousands of people and change world history, and the hardships he faced growing up were his training ground for that mission. Moreover, he had no way of knowing that as he engaged in the childhood that led him to his destiny, so did another young boy living in Germany, and their worlds were bound to collide.

The Making of The Liberator

John Galione standing in the Harriman section of Bristol, PA.

Chapter 2

The Corresponding Rise of the Rocket and the Reich

Imagine a little boy so enthralled with the universe that he spent a lifetime turning his toy rocket into a spaceship, only to be seduced by the German Army to convert his rocket ship into the most powerful weapon made for war—the world's first ballistic missile—*Hitler's secret weapon!* Much worse, mass-producing this weapon for the German Army required the creation of an entire city built around a top-secret rocket factory, and the most horrifying Nazi slave labor operation of World War II. It's hard to fathom that an operation so dreadful began with a young German boy who dreamed of building the spaceships he read about in science fiction novels.

The boy whose passion for space entwined him with the Nazis was Wernher von Braun. Von Braun was born on March 23, 1912, in Wirsitz, Germany. He performed his first rocket experiment at the age of twelve by strapping six large rockets to a red toy wagon and igniting them. With streaming flames and a cloud of smoke, the wagon shot five blocks down the street as townspeople dashed for cover. The police arrived to witness the "Grand Finale" explosion in the middle of Tiergarten Strasse, the most affluent part of town. A later experiment caused uproar when his rocket crashed through the window of a local bakery. Over time, people circulated petitions in an effort to ban the rockets.

At the age of seventeen von Braun joined the Society for Space Travel (*Verein für Raumschiffahrt* or "VfR") in Breslau. His favorite author, Professor Hermann Oberth, was president of the society. Oberth was working to prove that liquid fuel would more powerfully thrust a rocket into space than the usual solid fuel propellant, black powder. He designed what was considered to be the world's first liquid-fueled rocket motor, the *Kegeldüse* (*nose cone*). By summer of 1930, Oberth performed an elaborate demonstration of the motor in the presence of the director of the Chemical and Technical Institute. The director certified the demonstration, documenting for the first time in Germany the liquid-fueled rocket motor as "a respectable member of the family of internal-combustion engines."

Ironically, only weeks before the team began working on the rocket motor, Lt. Col. Karl Emil Becker of the German Army Ordnance decided to revive the rocket as a weapon for war. Colonel Becker made the crafty decision because the June 28, 1919, Treaty of Versailles forbade Germany to have cannons or guns with a three-inch bore; however, the treaty failed to mention rockets. Becker took advantage of the oversight by establishing a rocket program for the German Army.

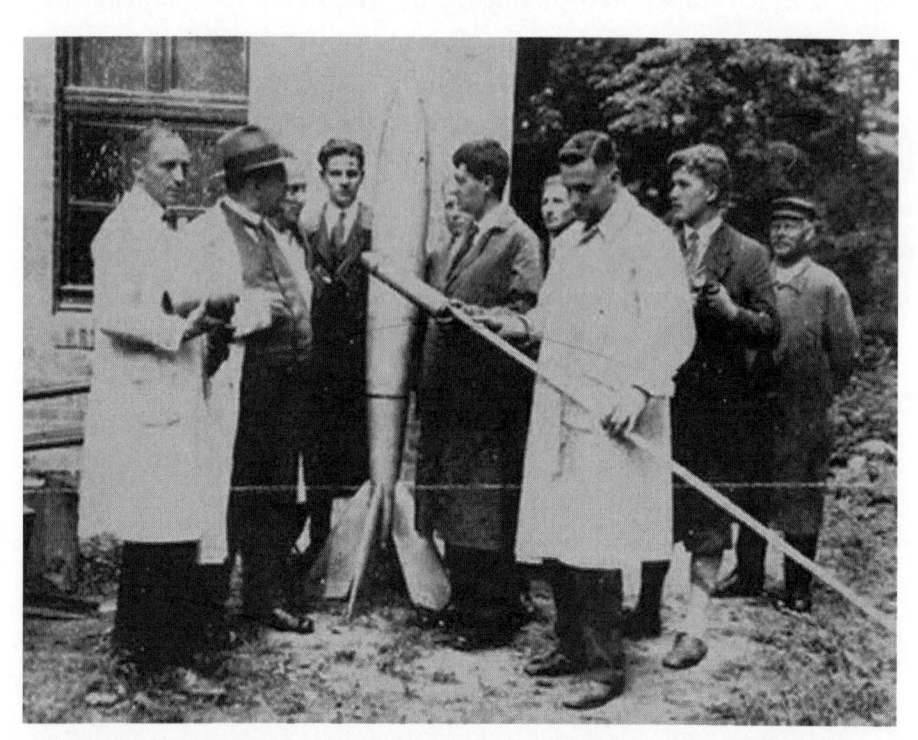

Professor Oberth's team holding Kegelduse rockets. Left to right: Rudolf Nebel, Dr. Ritter, Mr. Baermueller, Kurt Heinish, Hermann Oberth, Klaus Riedel, Wernher von Braun, and an unidentified man. (NASA-MSFC-6517791)

In September of 1930, von Braun and his team moved into a three-hundred-acre abandoned munitions dump located in the Berlin suburb of Reinickendorf and named it, Berlin Rocket Field (*Raketenflugplatz Berlin*). Coincidentally, within weeks Colonel Becker had chosen the Kummersdorf Artillery Proving Ground sixty miles south of Berlin for the Army's top-secret rocket center. With each team of scientists unaware of the other, the Society for Space Travel and the German Army began respective rocket programs.

Between spring and autumn of 1931, three rockets had been created and launched at the Rocket Field: the *Mirak*, the *Repulsor, and a* modified *pencil-shaped Repulsor*. The first two crashed into trees, but the modified Repulsor reached an altitude of over a thousand feet, and then returned to Earth by parachute. With the problem fixed, successful launches became usual and the VfR raised money by publicizing their "cutting edge technology on the brink of a breakthrough."

Although von Braun's endeavor to build the world's first spaceship seemed far removed from Hitler and the Nazi agenda, publicity caused their worlds to merge. In the spring of 1932, three high-ranking officials from Kummersdorf visited the rocket team. Colonel Becker, Major von Horstig, and Captain Walter Dornberger questioned the team on their progress with liquid-fueled rockets. The team revealed that they were the only people in Germany working to develop the technology. Dornberger realized their backyard operation was more technologically advanced than the military.

Eager to get liquid fuel rocket technology under military control, Becker offered von Braun 300 *marks* per month to develop rockets at Kummersdorf. Seduced by the prospect of getting paid for his rocket research, along with an endless supply of funds for building materials, plus the opportunity to work with state-of-the-art equipment, von Braun left the VfR to continue his work at the secret military rocket center at Kummersdorf Proving Ground.

KUMMERSDORF AND CHAOS

Von Braun's move to Kummersdorf placed an ominous twist on his life's ambition of building the world's first spaceship. At the Rocket Field, he had been developing rockets intended for space travel. At Kummersdorf, however, by November of 1932 he was in charge of developing top-secret missiles for the German War Machine!

Becker offered remaining VfR members an opportunity to work at Kummersdorf, but they declined to develop space vehicles under military control. Meanwhile, von Braun built his first rocket at Kummersdorf: a modified Repulsor capable of developing a thrust of 660 pounds. To his dismay, the rocket exploded. Dornberger renamed the Repulsor the *A-1* (Aggregate-1), as the first in a series of rocket developments perfected by trial and error, each effort becoming the sum of their research.

While von Braun worked on the Repulsor, Hitler became chancellor of Germany on January 30, 1933. Storm Troopers (SA) dressed in brown shirts paraded through the streets with torches. Hitler replaced members of the *Reichstag* (German Parliament) with members of the Nazi Party. Through the Nazi-dominated Reichstag, the Enabling Act was passed, giving Hitler the power to write his own laws and change the constitution. Hitler used his power to methodically strip Jews, Gypsies, Slavs, Communists, homosexuals, non-Aryans, and the handicapped of their rights, in an effort to remove them from society and replace them with his "Master Race."

Over the next 18 months civil liberties were taken away. Esterwegen, Brandenburg, and Dachau Concentration Camps were created. Jews were persecuted and beaten. A nationwide boycott was organized against their shops, and they were purged from the German Armed Forces. Non-Aryan doctors, pharmacists, and dentists were banned from practicing in German hospitals. The Gestapo was established as a state-authorized terror organization. Religious gatherings were banned. Books were burned. Hitler's Secret Police (SD) was created to spy on and capture anti-Nazis. Jews and Gypsies were forcibly sterilized, causing a massive exodus from Germany.

While Hitler attempted to take over those he deemed inferior, Ernst Röhm and his Storm Troopers tried to take over the Army. By the end of 1933, Röhm's SA had grown to a frightening 2.5 million strong, while Heinrich Himmler's SS were numbered at a mere 53,000. The conflict between the SA and the Army led to fighting in the streets. To prevent a civil war, President Hindenburg pressed Hitler for action. On the night of

June 30, 1934, Hitler radioed the code word *Kolibri* (German for "hummingbird") to Berlin, which signaled the SS to perform a massive blood purge of SA leadership, including Röhm who was shot in the head by two SS assassins. This historical event of mass murder is known as "The Night of the Long Knives." When the killing was over, the SS became independent of the SA and took control of their concentration camps.

Heinrich Himmler, who devised the entire operation, was promoted second to Hitler and placed in charge of the Gestapo. One month later President Hindenburg died. Hitler combined the offices of chancellor and president and declared himself Führer of Germany. Military officers were then required to pledge unconditional personal loyalty to Hitler. Despite the fact that in January Hitler had signed a non-aggression pact with Poland, he promptly announced the military draft and the resurrection of the *Luftwaffe* (German for "Air Force").

As Hitler rose in power, so did von Braun and his rockets. Two *A-2s* launched on December 19 and 20 reached an altitude of 6,500 feet—about one and a half miles. Then, an A-3 was created with an engine that packed 3,200 pounds of thrust. Success caused von Braun to initiate a massive joint venture between the German Army and Air Force. He proposed they build a top-secret joint Army-Air Force rocket research center where Army and Air Force engineers could collaborate on respective projects; and where rockets could be assembled and launched at the same center, in total seclusion, and out of the range of enemy surveillance. On April 1, 1936, Colonel Becker received permission to start building the secret installation on the island of Usedom at a virtually unknown place called, *Peenemünde*. Despite a massive effort to secure the perfect hiding place, Peenemünde eventually gave birth to a missile too big and powerful to hide from the enemies of Germany.

PEENEMÜNDE: THE BIRTH OF SUPERSONIC MISSILES

At 24-years-old, von Braun had accomplished a scientist's dream. His work with liquid fuel rocket technology had incited an infectious enthusiasm that spread from the Army to the Air Force and later enticed the

Navy. As a result, Germany spent millions of *marks* on building and populating an entire city centered on a top-secret joint Army-Air Force rocket research and manufacturing center. This enormous clandestine enterprise was based upon von Braun's research.

In April of 1937, all German rocket testing was transferred to "Army Experimental Station Peenemünde" to test-launch A-3 rockets. Launching the A-3 revealed a powerful propulsion system. When the design office opened in May, Technical Director von Braun and a hundred rocket specialists transferred to Peenemünde. Rocket Field veterans who had refused to work for the Army joined von Braun at Peenemünde, including a former associate, Arthur Rudolph. They developed rockets for the Army at Peenemünde-East, while Air Force engineers incorporated rocket technology into aircraft at Peenemünde-West. During this time, one could not move up professionally or politically without first joining the Nazi Party. Von Braun and several others had become members.

Barely six months after the design office opened, Hitler called a secret meeting on November 5, 1937, with the heads of the Armed Forces. Although Hitler had been declaring peace in public, this meeting historically known as the Hossbach Conference revealed his true plan to "preserve and enlarge Germany's racial community" by seizing Austria and Czechoslovakia, and waging war with France and England in order to expand Germany's *Lebensraum* (German for "living space").

From the early 1920s on, Hitler calculated expanding Germany's living space by conquering other nations, ridding the acquired land of Jews and others he deemed inferior, and repopulating the land with his "Master Race." From anti-Semitic propaganda designed to turn the public against Jews, to passing laws making it illegal for Jews and non-Aryans to live and work in Germany, to the terror imposed by Hitler's Special Forces commissioned to throw his "undesirables" into designated areas and concentration camps, all were part of a massive, comprehensive plan to fulfill this agenda. Hitler believed so strongly in a predominately Germanic society that he informed leaders of the Armed Forces that upon his death they were to carry out his plan as his last will and testament.

The Corresponding Rise of the Rocket and the Reich

By the time Hitler revealed his diabolical plan to the heads of the German Armed Forces, the *Lebensborn* breeding program had been operating for two years. German women deemed "racially pure" had begun having the babies of Aryan SS officers. Buchenwald and other camps steadily filled up with Jews, Communists, and anti-Nazis. Hitler hated Communists, as he believed 75-percent of them were Jews. Thousands of Polish Jews had been deported. Many fled. But the worst was yet to come.

Meanwhile, by February 4 Hitler had replaced all leaders who opposed him and proclaimed himself "Supreme Commander of the Armed Forces." In light of Hitler's plan to conquer large portions of Europe, the Army realized Germany's need for a weapon that could cross the ocean and inflict mass-destruction on large populations. Standing up to the challenge, Becker charged von Braun to deliver a missile that could double the range of the 76-mile-range Paris Gun, while carrying a one-ton warhead downrange to its target.

To cross the ocean, the rocket would have to break the sound barrier when none had yet reached supersonic speed, and the guidance system needed perfecting. Von Braun responded to the challenge by gathering the brightest minds of Germany to brainstorm, research, and experiment "under one roof" in the fields of engineering, aerodynamics, mathematics, guidance, and radio-control. They created departments and personnel in their respective fields. Innovative engineers and scientists made the necessary changes to von Braun's developments that empowered the rocket to unprecedented speed, stability, and accuracy.

In the summer of 1938, Dornberger was placed in charge of a new section called, Ordnance Test 11. From then on, a massive effort was made to create the world's first ballistic missile, its manufacturing facility, the city in which its employees will live, and the power station that runs the trains that bring them to and from work. They planned to have the factory built and ready to mass-produce the rockets by the time the A-4 was finished being developed in 1943.

However, this enormous project would require 9,000 construction workers and cost more than 180-million *marks*. Hitler's rating system decided how much money, material, and manpower to put toward each project. For the rocket team to obtain such resources, the development project and the factory project would have to achieve a simultaneous "Top Priority" rating. But Hitler refused to grant that rating without first being convinced of the rocket's potential.

Chemical Engineer and Propulsion Department head, Walter Thiel, proved the rocket's potential. He developed the 25-metric-ton engine (55,000-pound-thrust motor) that brought the A-4 to supersonic speed. Over the years, more than 60,000 drawings were made; parts were handcrafted, modified, and tested. Thiel's innovations made the engine so powerful that the combustion chamber melted upon ignition, creating the need to invent "film cooling." Specialist Moritz Pohlmann discovered that spreading a film of alcohol fuel along the wall of the combustion chamber worked as an insulator between the chamber and extreme heat from burning gasses.

In addition, Dr. Max Schirmer's heat transfer research resulted in using special steel to prevent heat problems during the rocket's reentry into the atmosphere. Ernst Steinhoff's guidance team developed the *Vertikant* guidance system, featuring radio equipment that cut off the engine at correct velocity. To test rockets, Dr. Rudolf Hermann, Dr. Hermann Kurzweg, and their aerodynamics department built the largest and most advanced wind tunnel in the world. Mechanisms that brought the A-4 to fruition were developed in an *A-5* test-rocket. They dropped A-5 rockets from an Air Force bomber 23,000 feet in the air. As the rockets fell to the ground and broke the sound barrier, they were photographed and studied. Fins were then made to steady the rocket. By October 1938 the first unguided A-5s were successfully launched and were test-launched horizontally and vertically throughout 1939. (This and more extensive information on the creation of the ballistic missile is found in an excellent book entitled, *The Rocket and the Reich,* by Michael Neufeld.)

**A-4 rockets moving and launching at Peenemünde
(AMCOM, United States Army Redstone Arsenal)**

As the rocket team advanced in missile technology, terror increased in Germany. Exactly one year after the Hossbach Conference, on November 6, 1938, a young Polish Jew had killed a German diplomat in retaliation for sending his parents to a concentration camp. Three nights later Nazi Storm Troopers took revenge on Jewish shops, synagogues, and people. While on a violent rampage, they shattered the windows of Jewish businesses and burned their buildings to the ground. Dozens of Jews were beaten or killed. Hundreds were thrown into concentration camps. This night of terror is known as *Kristallnacht* (German for "Night of the Broken Glass").

Barely two weeks after the annexation of Austria and Czechoslovakia, and while planning the invasion of Poland, Hitler visited Kummersdorf on March 27, 1939, to see if the A-4 was ready for war, but the rocket needed further development. Immediately after touring the plant Hitler informed Britain he wanted to go to war with Poland, but on March 31 Britain announced their unconditional support of Poland. Nevertheless, Hitler sent 2,600 tanks and 2,000 aircraft into Poland on September 1, 1939. Two days later France and England joined the war in Poland's defense. Millions of Jewish and non-Jewish Poles were killed. Thousands were thrown into concentration camps and ghettos. Going to war earlier than planned caused a munitions crisis that led Colonel Becker to committed suicide. In the meantime, von Braun joined the SS.

Over time, Hitler conquered Belgium, Holland, Luxembourg, and France. When Britain held out, he ordered the *Luftwaffe* to bomb British airfields, starting the Battle of Britain. On June 22, 1941, Hitler broke his non-aggression pact with Moscow and invaded the Soviet Union. Special killing forces (*Einsatzgruppen*) assigned to find and kill Jews, Soviet officials, and Gypsies followed advancing troops, killing approximately 700,000 Jews by the end of 1941, with a total of 1.2-million people brutally murdered by the end of war. As with Poland, remaining Jews and political prisoners were thrown into concentration camps and ghettos. Over 1.5-million soldiers were taken prisoner. By this time the SS had grown to over 250,000 strong!

French Resistance members worked fearlessly to thwart the Nazi effort. They blew up train cars carrying German equipment. They hid Jews and anti-Nazis to keep them from being transported to concentration camps, giving them false papers to ensure their escape. These heroes did everything possible to impede the Nazi agenda, saving thousands of lives. Unfortunately, the Nazi force had grown too large to stop. Many Resistance members were captured and executed, or tortured in concentration camps.

Interestingly, changing tides of the war ensured the demise of Germany. After the December 7 attack on Pearl Harbor, President Roosevelt declared war on Japan. Japan told Hitler they would break their non-aggression pact with the Soviet Union if Hitler declared war on the United States. On December 11, Hitler misjudged Japan's willingness to break the pact and declared war on the United States—*the move that sealed the fate of Hitler's Third Reich!* Japan reneged, leaving the Soviet Union and the United States free to crush Germany as respective troops advanced from the East and West. Germany did not have the resources to win a war against both Russia and the United States without Japan's aid.

Despite Germany's inevitable defeat, the Nazis continued working toward their goal of eradicating European Jews. On January 20, 1942, fifteen high-ranking Nazis at a conference in Wannsee (a district of Berlin) decided the Final Solution to achieving this goal was through either forced sterilization or annihilation through work. The plan was to send Jews to labor camps, where large populations could "die of natural causes." In the early 1940s the SS had begun secretly building labor camps. Jews and foreign workers were arrested for trivial offenses, thrown in the camps, and forced to work under inhuman conditions. Himmler later determined the Final Solution would include Jewish children in order to prevent them from later avenging their parents' deaths.

From the invasion of Poland on, death camps were set up for the purpose of eliminating European Jews. By spring of 1942, Heinrich Himmler had placed a high-raking air ministry construction employee, Hans Kammler, in charge of building the death camps and gas chambers of Birkenau, Belzec, Treblinka, and others. Then, on July 19, Himmler ordered all Jews in Poland sent to death camps by the end of the year. Four days later the first transports from Warsaw ghetto arrived at Treblinka. By October 4, all Jews in concentration camps were ordered to Auschwitz, where approximately 9,000 people died daily in massive Zyklon-B poison gassings.

It seemed the world had gone mad. While thousands of innocent victims were brought to the gas chambers in the spring of 1942, the A-4 weapon of mass destruction was brought to the test stands. On October 3, the 46-foot-high A-4 rocket shot 52 miles into the sky, traveled 116 miles in distance at 4,400 feet per second, and landed within 2.5 miles of its target. At a subsequent celebration Dornberger announced the birth of the first spaceship:

"We have invaded space with our rocket and for the first time . . . we have proved rocket propulsion practicable for space travel. This third day of October, 1942, is the first of a new era of transportation that of space travel."

General Erich Fellgiebel congratulates Colonel Leo Zanssen (center) for the First successful A-4 flight. Dornberger stands in front of von Braun (fourth from left); Wind tunnel expert, Dr. Rudolf Hermann, smiling (second from right). (NASA-MSFC-9131999)

As a result of the successful launch Hitler endorsed the rocket late November. By December 5 he ordered Speer to set up the *A-4 Special Committee* and appointed a zealous Nazi, Gerhard Degenkolb, supervisor of the committee. On December 22, Hitler signed an order for the mass production of the A-4 missile. By January he gave the A-4 priority over their radar program. In February, the head of labor supply, a man named Jaeger, suggested using Russian POWs for missile production, and then later proposed using concentration camp inmates. A small concentration camp was built at Peenemünde in the basement of building F-1.

In March, three subcontractors were chosen to begin producing 300 rockets per month by December 1943. Production sites were created at Peenemünde, Zeppelin Airship Construction in Friedrichshafen, and Rax-Werke locomotive factory in Wiener Neustadt, Austria. The Friedrichshafen camp was a branch camp of Dachau. Prisoners there made A-4 propellant tanks and midsection fuselages. Degenkolb's former company, DEMAG in Berlin-Falkensee, was considered as a fourth site. On April 12, Arthur Rudolph toured Heinkel Aircraft and returned confident over using slave labor for missile production, since Heinkel had "only the best experiences with them." They had acquired 4,000 forced laborers in only eight months. Rudolph believed using slaves insured secrecy, as prisoners have no contact with the outside world.

Unbeknownst to Rudolph, the secret was already out. Britain had become aware of the giant missiles when one of them accidentally blew up over Switzerland and the British confiscated the debris for study. Then, vapor trails from test launchings alerted British Intelligence of the exact location of the missile program. On April 15, Intelligence informed England's Prime Minister, Winston Churchill, that the Germans were developing powerful, long-range rockets for the purpose of attacking Britain. On May 26, 1943, the A-4 made its first successful flight going a distance of 159 miles, and only three miles off target. The Army's challenge to "double the range of the Paris Gun" had been met—*and more!*

From April to June, Arthur Rudolph and others worked to fill all plant locations with thousands of slave laborers. Hundreds of Russian war prisoners were sent by train to work in maintenance. Many were from Buchenwald and Mauthausen Concentration Camps. By the end of April, Peenemünde (East and West) had obtained more than 3,000 foreign prisoners. Inmates at F-1 were forced to install the barbed wire fencing that surrounded their prison. As inmates arrived into all locations, the Royal Air Force (RAF) met on June 29 to study reconnaissance photos of the Peenemünde complex. Since A-4 rockets traveled too fast to shoot down with anti-aircraft guns, under the code name of Operation Hydra they planned a strategic attack on the entire rocket research center.

While RAF bombers devised the details of the attack, Dornberger and von Braun presented an elaborate propaganda film of the A-4 program to Hitler, in the hope of gaining full financial support for their missile. Hitler agreed to examine the film in his last hope of winning the war. During the film, von Braun described how he and his team had created everything: from the crane that serviced the rocket—to the Meillerwagen cart that carried it to its launching pad—to the intricate workings of the first supersonic missile. Slow motion was used to grip the Führer during the most thrilling parts of the film. The final impact was brought to a climax with the words, "We made it after all!"

After the film, Hitler became obsessed. He asked von Braun to increase the warhead from one ton to ten tons. When Dornberger explained the modification would cost another five years at the drawing board, Hitler became insistent: *"But I want annihilation!"* Dornberger assured Hitler that raising the warhead was not necessary since the world had "no defense against such a swift and powerful rocket." Hitler was so elated he made von Braun a professor. "The A-4 is a measure that can decide the war," he later enthused in his bunker to Albert Speer. "This is the decisive weapon of the war . . . you must push the A-4 as hard as you can." On July 8 Hitler ordered Speer to set the A-4 project in parity with tank production, giving it Top Priority over all other armaments projects. He insisted on 5,000 units as soon as possible so he could "force England to her knees" with a simultaneous strike of all 5,000 missiles!

"From the end of July on, tremendous industrial capacity was diverted to the huge missile," said Albert Speer in his book, *Inside the Third Reich*. Propaganda Minister, Josef Goebbels, touted a "wonder weapon" would soon appear. The ballistic missile had become the most important project of the Third Reich. Hitler ordered Speer to quickly supply all the materials needed to mass-produce the missile. Hitler's only stipulation was for the administration to fill the missing manpower with only German workers. "God help us if the enemy finds out about the business," he said. But on July 11, Hitler's order was quietly ignored with the arrival of 400 mostly French prisoners in Peenemünde. By July 16 they had begun assembling

A-4 midsections. On August 4, Arthur Rudolph made the decision to bring in concentration camp inmates at a ratio of 10 to 15 prison inmates to every German worker. Inmates filled into all locations.

By summer of 1943, Peenemünde had grown to include barracks, office buildings, machine shops, a rocket factory, a liquid-oxygen manufacturing plant, wind tunnels and test stands that could withstand incredible thrust; railroads and tramcars, clubs and sports arenas, apartments and town houses, warehouses, and a new harbor to better receive coal shipments. It had become a paradise where 12,000 employees worked; 6,000 of them were scientists and engineers working at Peenemünde-East. All wore identification badges showing the departments for which they had clearance. Peenemünde had evolved into a massive Army-Air Force rocket and jet engine center where in five years innovative research and development performed under von Braun's direction had produced astonishing breakthroughs in missile technology. So astonishing, Navy Submarine Commander, Fritz Steinhoff, asked von Braun to design, build, and test a six-solid-fuel rocket torpedo for submarines that von Braun said "would have revolutionized sea warfare" by enabling the Navy to blast a shore target. However, fierce competition between the armed forces ceased the torpedo project.

Nevertheless, the A-4 program was discovered. In the dark early morning of August 18, 1943, harrowing explosions sent von Braun and Dornberger diving for shelter. Incredibly, 560 Royal Air Force bombers roared through a moonlit sky, dropping 1,800 tons of bombs on the installation at Peenemünde. The bombers had been ordered not to return until the rocket center was completely destroyed. Mosquito flights worked to divert German night fighters to Berlin while Master Bomber Captain J. H. Searby of the 83rd Squadron marked crucial targets at Peenemünde. With red flares he led the way for 4,000 men to attack crucial areas of the rocket center.

The first wave of attack was aimed at the scientists, but one-third of their explosives accidentally hit concentration camp inmates. The second wave was aimed at the rocket factory, and the third wave was aimed at the administrative offices. When the bombing was over, 180 Germans had been killed, including Walther Thiel and many other main rocket scientists. The RAF suffered a loss of 40 aircraft with crew: 23 Lancasters, 15 Halifaxes, and two Stirlings. Sadly, about 750 forced laborers were killed. Inmates who escaped the bombing had no idea that the inmates who perished were the fortunate ones; for the prisoners who survived the bombing of Peenemünde were about to experience the most horrible, living hell.

Chapter 3

The Nightmare of Camp Dora and War

The Royal Air Force bombing left Peenemünde in ruins and killed many of the main rocket scientists, including Walther Thiel. But the technology that gave birth to the world's first supersonic missile had already been created and the Germans were eager to mass-produce the weapon regardless of the human cost. In a series of secret meetings Hitler, Himmler, Speer, and Dornberger planned to revive the rocket program. Heinrich Himmler recommended they (1) move the A-4 production site "underground" where Hitler's secret weapon could be safely mass-produced away from the threat of bombings, (2) place death camp construction chief, Hans Kammler, in charge of erecting the new facilities, and (3) use only concentration camp slave labor to produce the rocket. Using prison inmates ensured secrecy, since they have no contact with the outside world. "Such prisoners did not even have any mail," Himmler said. "This will be the largest and most important armaments task that the Führer could assign."

It was bad enough that the SS was in charge of supplying slave labor from Buchenwald and other camps for rocket production; now the fate of the prisoners would be in the hands of the man responsible for the innovation of the gas chambers of Auschwitz-Birkenau, Treblinka, Belzec, and Majdanek! Although Albert Speer considered Kammler to be a "cold, ruthless schemer, a fanatic in the pursuit of a goal, and as carefully calculating as he was unscrupulous," they worked together to restore the missile program.

In a top-secret meeting on August 26, 1943, Kammler, Speer, and Dornberger chose to move A-4 production to a chemical weapons reserve 130 miles southwest of Berlin. Production would take place deep within a labyrinth of secret underground tunnels running through the Harz Mountains of Thuringia, near the city of Nordhausen. Two main tunnels, Tunnel A and Tunnel B, forty feet wide by twenty-eight feet high ran parallel through the base of the mountain. Tunnels A and B were connected by forty-seven cross-tunnels 150-yards long numbered zero through 46. The camp was established as a Buchenwald sub-camp. Production of the secret missile would take place in hidden cross-tunnel chambers under the codename *"Dora."*

Dual railroad tracks linked directly to the German railway system ran through the tunnels, ensuring the surreptitious shipping and receiving of rockets and rocket parts. The government company that hollowed out Tunnel B from the northern to the southern side of the mountain (over a mile deep) had not finished excavating Tunnel A. Sadly, the arduous task of excavating Tunnel A's caves of solid granite fell upon the prisoners of Buchenwald and other camps, including the inmates who survived the bombing of Peenemünde.

Two days later, the first 107 prisoners transferred from Buchenwald to Tunnel A to begin moving chemical drums out of the tunnel to prepare for building the factory. Over time, a steady stream of Russian, French, Polish, Czechoslovakian, Italian, and German political prisoners arrived in the tunnels for work. Many Jews came later. Inmates were assigned to *Commandos* (work teams) of forty men. Camp leaders created a malicious work environment by placing common criminals called *Capos* in charge of the prisoners.

Inmates performed backbreaking work on twelve-to eighteen-hour rotating shifts on a ration of one piece of bread, a smidgen of margarine, and a cup of greenish black chicory water. Sometimes they received a thin soup with a small piece of sausage or potato. Prisoners loaded equipment and chemical drums onto railcars, while under the brutal blows of the SS and Capos. Taskmasters ordering them to work faster and faster beat them with clubs and rubber-tipped twisted copper cables. Laborers had no running water to quench their thirst, no washing facilities to sooth their wounds. Desperate inmates bathed in urine and licked condensation to quench their thirst. Chemical drums cut in half became makeshift latrines, causing an unbearable stench in the tunnels.

On September 24, the Speer ministry established a state-owned company to manufacture the missile under the stealthy name of *Mittelwerk*

GmbH (German for "Central Works Limited"). In October they received a contract for the manufacture of nine hundred A-4 units per month, up to a maximum of twelve thousand rockets per year. Detainees from Peenemünde were transported to the Mittelwerk, along with machinery from the factory. The Germans made them march naked from the railroad station in order to discourage escape. While some inmates excavated the tunnels, others erected missile production machinery in the Mittelwerk factory.

From October to April, prisoners worked and slept in cold, damp tunnels barely lit by mining lanterns and low-wattage bulbs. Inmates came out into the sunlight only during Sunday roll call. As a result, many suffered impaired vision. When their shift ended, exhausted men slept in the tunnels on smelly lice-and scabies-infested straw bedding shared by the previous shift. Although there had been an order to build a barracks camp outside the tunnel, Kammler was too obsessed with raising the factory to stop and build a place for the prisoners to sleep. "Pay no attention to the human cost," he said. "The work must go ahead, and in the shortest possible time."

Eventually, the SS ordered prisoners to erect wooden bunks four levels high in cross-tunnels 43 to 46. Several inmates slept crowded head-to-foot in each bunk. Sometimes bunks came crashing down, killing frail men below. Prisoners, afraid of being crushed or thrown off their beds by Russian bullies slept on bare rock in tunnels that averaged a constant 56°F. Those excavating the mountain suffered the most physically punishing work. Inmates were forced to break through solid granite with pickaxes, jackhammers, and their bare hands. Exhausted laborers trying to sleep in the tunnels were driven insane by the constant commotion. Jean Michel, who came to live and work in the tunnels of Camp Dora on October 14, describes the unbearable scenario in his book, *DORA*:

> The noise bores into the brain and shears the nerves. The demented rhythm lasts for 15 hours. Arriving at the dormitory as the Capos hurry us along with blows, we do not even try to reach the bunks. Drunk with exhaustion, we collapse onto the rocks . . . Soon, over a thousand despairing men, at the limit of their resistance and racked with thirst, lie there hoping for sleep which never comes; for the shouts of the guards, the noise of

machines, the explosions and the ringing of the bell reach them even there. Some prisoners went mad . . . all of it echoing mercilessly in the closed world of the tunnel.

Having no safety equipment, inmates suffered serious injuries or were crushed and killed under falling boulders. To remove foreign objects from bodies, they had to perform surgeries using "medieval anesthesia"—a bang on the head. On October 20, a missile-testing site was established. Large caves were hollowed out to cathedral height deep in the air-deprived tunnels. Prisoners, too weak to work with pickaxes held above their heads, cried as they collapsed to their death from high scaffolding. "A cry, a thud, that is all," wrote Michel, "another man takes the victim's place."

As winter set in, inmates were forced to stand at attention for several hours in wind, rain, and freezing cold weather wearing thin prison clothes and wooden clogs, as SS guards called out a list of over five thousand people. Those who collapsed endured brutal beatings; others were shot or tortured. After roll call, the prisoners were made to run soaking wet into the damp tunnels to begin working. Insufficient food, water, and sanitation, combined with brutality and the cold of winter, triggered outbreaks of epidemics and raised the death toll. Muscle men known for their strength and vitality quickly became weak and emaciated. In October, eighteen prisoners had died. In December 679 died. By the end of December, nearly eleven thousand sick and emaciated people worked and slept in the damp tunnels. One prisoner actually went insane from weeks of excessive thirst. He died in agony after gulping down rocket fuel.

After visiting the Mittelwerk factory on December 8, Dr. Poschmann, the head physician, told Albert Speer he had seen *Dante's Inferno*. French survivor, Jean Mialet, offered a similar statement: "This is what hell must be like," he said. According to camp records, Speer inspected the underground tunnels on December 10. In his book, *Infiltration*, he describes the prisoners as having "expressionless faces" and "exhausted bodies." That same day, Speer ordered the construction of barracks to be built in the valley on the southern side of the hill about 750 meters from Tunnel B. His motive was to improve conditions in order to increase missile production speed and accuracy.

While barracks were being built, prisoners were made to build Dora sub-camps Ellrich and Harzungen (Mittelwerk II and Mittelwerk III). Many more deaths occurred as they hollowed out various caves under the most inhumane conditions. Before the portable crematorium was brought to Dora in January, corpses were sent to the Buchenwald crematorium to be burned. Camp records show that upon learning of their impending transfer to Camp Dora, prisoners of Buchenwald who were horrified by the smashed bodies coming in from Dora simply killed themselves first, before ever having to board the transport wagons.

Michel Depierre, a French Resistance member who was arrested by the Gestapo and sent to Buchenwald, filled with despair when he learned of his impending transfer to Camp Dora. Depierre wrote in his memoir: "I got really depressed when I learned that I'm leaving for the Camp of Dora to work in the underground factory . . . only dead comes back from Dora in wagons and trucks to be burned in the crematorium of Buchenwald."

When inmates saw the massive A-4 missile for the first time, they feared the Germans planned to use them to destroy the world. When the time came to begin assembling the rockets, brave prisoners formed an underground resistance. They risked their lives by inflicting upon the missiles all conceivable methods of sabotage. Inmates urinated on wiring, loosened bolts, faked welds, used faulty parts, and arranged flawed connections.

In January the first fifty-two missiles that came off the assembly line sorely malfunctioned. Camp Commandant, Otto Forschner, immediately issued a warning of sabotage punishable by death. Prisoners then endured brutal beatings and daily mass hangings in the most grisly manner. To prolong suffering and death, prisoners' hands and feet were tied with electric cables, wood was shoved in their mouths and secured with wire tied behind their necks, and then they were hung on the roll call grounds.

Retired Belgian Army Officer, Rene Steenbeke, describes the brutal method of hanging: "I saw fifty-one prisoners being hanged, their hands behind their backs, a piece of wood in their mouths, hanged in groups of about twelve. They could see their comrades being killed before them and they had to watch."

On March 9, inmates frightened to death by the daily mass hangings on the roll call square faked a brawl in their prison cell in an attempt to escape on a day when all but one guard had gone out for supper. When the SS guard opened the door the prisoners knocked him unconscious and released other inmates. As they rushed toward freedom, the guard regained consciousness and fired his gun to alert the watchtower guards. Terrified inmates were mowed down with machine guns. Those who escaped were hunted down with vicious dogs and killed. Reprisals followed with mass executions, their bodies left to hang on the roll call ground in order to intimidate prisoners.

According to Dr. Karsten Uhl of the Mittelbau Dora Museum, by March of 1944 twenty-nine hundred inmates had died at Dora from dysentery, tuberculoses, pneumonia, pleurisy, anthrax, typhus, malnutrition, dehydration, and physical exhaustion. A permanent crematorium was installed to more efficiently dispose of the dead. Another three thousand too weak to work had been transported to death camps and gassed. The first two thousand went to Lublin-Majdanek in Poland and a thousand went to Bergen-Belsen. When people died, they were replaced with an endless supply of fresh victims from Buchenwald and other camps.

In March and April the outside barracks were completed. For the first time in months, prisoners began coming out of the damp tunnels into the warm sunshine to sleep in barracks made of green weatherboard. However, so many people were sickly from living in the tunnels for months that a crematorium Commando was formed in May. During this time, the first Hungarian Jews were transported to Dora. Then, Dornberger, von Braun, Rudolph, and Sawatzki called a meeting to discuss the transfer of eighteen hundred more French prisoners from Buchenwald.

The French Resistance had worked closely with Allied Intelligence, delivering vital information that helped bring to fruition Operation Overlord. On June 6, 1944, the D-day soldiers landed on the beaches of Normandy. Floating concrete blocks codenamed "Mulberries" allowed for vast supplies of men and equipment to be swiftly brought ashore. Had it not been for the RAF bombing of Peenemünde, which delayed rocket production for several months, the V-2 rockets would have destroyed the crucial Mulberry Harbor. Without supplies and reinforcements, the assault would have been doomed. Meanwhile, ailing prisoners struggled to survive on the hope of being rescued and returned to their families. Dora survivor and French Resistance veteran, Yves Beón, reveals in his book, *Planet Dora,* their desperate prayer:

> Here, believers and atheists meet in the same communion, begging God, even the devil, and all the genius that may come to the hearts of men to inject into the Americans that madness that will make them plunge forward enough to free us. Don't lose any time, guys, we're here crying out for help and you should hear us well. You, Harry, even if you have an ache in your side, charge on in spite of it! And you, Joe, even if your tank runs out of gas, push it with every ounce of strength! Even if you're tired, keep on as if nothing had happened, without stopping, so long as you arrive here! You'll have all the time you want to sleep afterward!

As the American Army advanced, the German guards at Dora became perturbed, bringing down their clubs upon prisoners for the slightest offense. Oddly, SS guards were greedy with the abuse of their prisoners. After a camp doctor complained that civilian workers had been beating or stabbing detainees with sharp objects, a decree was issued June 22 reminding employees that the privilege of punishing the inmates was reserved solely for the SS. Although conditions were horrible, the death rate declined in the summer of 1944 to 150 per month due to warmer weather and sleeping outside the tunnels. With another transport from Buchenwald arriving in July, camp population reached 11, 675 people working in the tunnels, preparing missiles for deployment.

In August, Himmler granted Kammler full authority to accelerate A-4 deployment. Kammler immediately set up a "Vengeance" division. Goebbels renamed the A-4 ballistic missile *Vergeltungswaffe Zwei-2* (German for "vengeance weapon number two" nicknamed "V-2"). He touted Hitler's new wonder weapon would soon bring Germany to victory. Hitler knew the V-1 cruise missile was too slow and noisy to win the war; however, the A-4/V-2 ballistic missile could quietly approach the enemy at supersonic speed while traveling too swiftly to be shot down by antiaircraft guns. The unmatched speed and destructive nature of the V-2 missile guaranteed Hitler the total annihilation required to conquer lands and breed his "Master Race."

Upon Kammler's orders, at 6:43 p.m. on Friday September 8, 1944, the first V-2 missile was fired from Holland and crossed the English Channel, traveling a distance of two hundred miles in only six minutes. The missile exploded on Staverly Road in the quiet suburb of Cheswick, West London, destroying six homes, injuring seventeen, and killing three people. Although Hitler had planned to simultaneously fire five thousand missiles at London, the first twenty-five missiles were fired over a period of ten days. The V-2 offensive continued for months and terrorized London, Paris, Belgium and Antwerp Harbor (the major delivery port for Allied equipment), injuring and killing thousands. The successful bombing of West London encouraged the SS to frantically expedite production. Additional laborers were brought in to manufacture missiles. From assembly to inspection, inmates struggled to work faster on the "hot job" producing up to seven hundred rockets per month. From October on, they were distraught that the D-day soldiers had not yet come to free them.

With a population of over twelve thousand people the camp grew large enough to separate from Buchenwald. By November, Dora had become a concentration camp in its own right with over three-dozen sub-camps under its new name, "Mittelbau Dora Concentration Camp." Having over a million square feet of floor space, Dora had become the largest underground factory in the world! Incredibly, the Mittelbau complex consisted of an eight thousand-square-kilometer restricted zone surrounded by two electrified fences and guard towers manned by SS guards with machine guns at the ready. (Mittelbau refers to the entire complex of factories and sub-camps within its boundaries.)

Other guards patrolled the tunnels with German Shepherds trained to attack upon command. The restricted zone included a huge roll call ground, the gallows, a kitchen, washrooms, bunker prison cells, a crematorium, a sports ground, cinema, and a brothel; factories for the manufacture of jet engines, workshops, the V-1 cruise missile, the V-2 ballistic missile, a liquid oxygen plant, manufacturing sites under the code names of Schlier, Lehesten, and Zement. Camp Dora even had its own money.

The Nightmare of Camp Dora and War

Should an Allied soldier find Camp Dora he would have hit the "Mother Lode" of Germany's War Machine!

With enormous operations of the world's most technological weaponry and jet engines being manufactured in the underground tunnels, secrecy was of the highest importance. Informants placed in the camp in May penetrated and uncovered the underground resistance by the end of October. On November 1 the SS began throwing resistance leaders into the "bunker" or Gestapo prison in Nordhausen, where they were interrogated, tortured, and hung on the roll call square.

The bunker was a one-story stone building containing thirty small cells, a cellar, two quarters for SS guards, and an interrogation room. In each six-by-eight-foot bunker cell, nineteen inmates were kept naked in order to discourage escape. Bunker prisoners died in agony during cruel interrogations. Abraham Biderman was transported to Dora the first week of February, unjustly thrown in the bunker, and interrogated under the threat of vice-grips until his body trembled with fright. Since Jews were given the worst jobs at Dora, Abraham was in charge of the waste bucket. In his book, *The World of My Past*, Biderman describes his daily routine in the bunker prison that he refers to as "the most frightening place at Dora. The House of No Return."

> Early in the morning the light came on and the prisoners turned around to face the door . . . we charged forward like race horses released from a starting box, hardly waiting for the command, 'Alle Raus! Los!' The corridor leading to the washrooms at the other end of the prison was long and narrow. Lined up on both sides, holding rubber truncheons and rubber-covered electric cables, the SS whipped us mercilessly as we ran past . . . By the time I got to the washroom I had collected lashes from every guard in the corridor. My whole body was covered in welts. I soon learned how to dodge some of the guards but the dogs were unavoidable. Going for my feet, they scared the life out of me. By the time I had cleaned and disinfected the container, I had to run back, having missed out on my chance to wash and, even more importantly, the chance of a drink I so desperately needed.

PENETRATING DARK FORCES

During the week of D-day, John Galione was drafted into the Army as a replacement soldier and sent to Camp Wheeler, Georgia. Sadly, most replacements died in battle due to their lack of training. While in combat training, Galione met a man named Steve Harmanos. The two men soon realized they shared a common background. Galione states:

> He was a cute little guy. His family used to call him Skeezo. He struck up the friendship. He liked hanging around me. He would always offer to help me with my chores. We were both quiet and shy, but once we talked we realized we had a lot in common. Both of our families had come from overseas and settled in America, we both came from big families with a lot of brothers, we were both raised on big Pennsylvania farms that were a large operation, and we were both of a Catholic background. We liked each other so much that we planned to stay friends after the war and get together with our families for many years. We made a pact with each other. We promised that if either one of us was killed in the war the other would go to the family and tell them he died brave.

John and Steve were shipped overseas in the fall of 1944. Upon arrival, Steve joined the 47th Infantry "Raider Regiment" of the 9th Infantry Division. John joined the 104th "Timberwolf" Army Infantry Division, 415th Regiment, Company B, 3rd Platoon, and became known as Private Galione. Private Galione and his comrades had been assigned the task of cleaning out the pillboxes (where Germans stashed explosives). One of his comrades mishandled a gun and accidentally shot the artillery, which set off a massive explosion. Exploding ammunition barely missed Private Galione, but killed and wounded many of his comrades, including the man next to him who had his legs blown off.

During the crossing of the Mark River in Holland, Galione, Leonard Puryear, and several other soldiers piled into a boat to cross the river. "The Germans were shelling the boats so badly," said Galione, "that we had to jump out and swim." Galione and the others from the 415th Infantry Regiment, Company B, swam across the river under fire. Although Galione was a good swimmer the weight of his backpack kept pushing his head under the water. "I thought about how my father used to carry two bushels of tomatoes on his shoulders for miles. I said to myself, 'If he could do it I could do it' and that gave me the determination I needed to keep my head above water."

When Galione and Puryear came ashore, they realized that they and a third man were the only three men who made it across the river alive out of their entire group. The rest of their comrades were killed. Exhausted, they took refuge as soon as they made it to shore. "We slept in a barn that night," said Galione. "But before going to sleep we talked about how strange it was to have been the only three who survived from our entire group."

"I don't know how I made it across," said Puryear. "I never learned how to swim." Galione and Puryear were amazed. After all, Galione was an excellent swimmer and nearly drowned. How did Puryear, who never swam a day in his life, make it across with a seventy-five-pound backpack? "We went to sleep that night with an overwhelming feeling that there was a divine reason we were the only three who survived out of so many men from our group who died crossing the river," said Galione.

Later, Galione and his comrades had advanced to Aachen, Germany. Upon arrival, they found themselves facing an entire line of German tanks blocking their advance. Galione took action: "I stood straight up in my jeep, took aim with my bazooka, and blew up the lead tank with a single round. Then, I and a few of my buddies jumped out of our vehicles, ran over to the tanks, and killed all the Germans attached to those tanks." According to both Galione and Sergeant Puryear, Galione's actions caused the entire line of tanks to retreat, enabling the Timberwolves to proceed into the heart of Germany. Private Galione received the Bronze Star for his actions and the nickname, Eagle Eye. Sergeant Puryear received the Silver Star. Nevertheless, the victory in Aachen was soon forgotten as December brought great sorrow. Private Galione and his buddy Steve Harmanos had made contact with each other on the battlefield. While facing a heavily defended factory district they took refuge in one of the buildings. Galione recalls the sad story:

There was a fierce battle. The Germans were on one side, and our tanks were coming up on the other side, bombing each building one after the other. The guys in our tanks didn't know we were in the building and our building was the next one to be bombed. We were trapped. We had to get out of there fast, but there was nowhere to run. We stood at the door trying to figure out where to go when Steve yelled out a plan. He had found a way for us to escape. "We'll run over here and then we'll go over there . . .," he said. It was a good plan, so I agreed; and we ran out the door together.

We were walking along the edge of a cliff. We stopped for a minute to decide which way to go and the next step he took was right on top of a land mine. I was standing right next to him when it happened. The land mine caused him to fall over the side of the cliff. I called out to him, but he died right away. You see, land mines were designed to maim and do damage. Falling in the ditch was a mercy because it caused him to die instantly, without suffering.

We had made a pact that if either one of us died the other would go to the family and tell them he died brave. The thing is: I wouldn't have to lie. He did die brave. His plan saved an entire platoon of men. I passed on his plan to the platoon and the whole platoon was able to escape because of Steve. The strange thing is that Steve never usually made the calls. He was quiet and shy. Here, this was the first time he had made a call and it caused his own death. It was so sad. He was such a nice guy.

Shortly after, the Timberwolves were stuck along the western banks of the flooded Roer River. Across the river, German soldiers were hiding in the dark with a Nazi officer, killing American soldiers coming ashore. At this point, Private Galione had lost contact with his squad and joined another squad of the 1st platoon. On February 23, 1945, he wiped out the enemy nest and single-handedly took them prisoner. Galione received the Bronze

Star with oak leaf cluster and a write-up in the newspaper. He and his regiment received the Distinguished (Presidential) Unit Citation for their accomplishment at the Roer River. Galione's Bronze Star citation states:

> Private Galione lost contact with his squad and joined another squad of his platoon. With three other men he set out to make contact with an adjoining platoon. Sighting four men standing in the darkness, Private Galione was unable to determine if they were Americans. Cautiously he crawled within a few yards of the men and was sighted and fired upon by a machine gun. Taking partial cover, he threw two hand grenades at the enemy position, wounding an officer and taking two of the enemy prisoner. His actions, which eliminated enemy opposition in the area, enabled his platoon to advance and seize its objective. The courage and superb devotion to duty displayed by Private Galione reflect great credit upon himself and the military service.

Meanwhile, Puryear had assumed the role of his sergeant when he became a casualty. Galione became an Army Scout whom Puryear allowed to investigate at will. If plagued by a gut feeling, Galione would leave word with his comrades to let the sarge know he had gone off on a scouting mission. "I'd scout for two or three days at a time and come back with information on the location of enemy nests," said Galione. "Then, I'd report their location to the sarge, he'd pass that information on to our platoon, and our whole platoon would go out and wipe out every one of those enemy nests." The sarge was always happy when I'd come back with information because it led to victory. He gained reputation and it earned our platoon a name." (The 3rd platoon was nicknamed, "The Fighting Platoon".) Private Galione was unaware that his scouting missions were sharpening an intuition that would send him on a heroic, 100-mile lone scouting mission through the most extreme Nazi territory in search of concetration camp prisoners.

CRUELTY INTENSIFIED

Fearing the Russian advance, from December to February Jews and Gypsies were entrained or death-marched to Dora from Auschwitz and Gross-Rosen. Dora had no gas chambers. Those too sick or weak to work were dumped in the Nordhausen Death Camp (Boelcke-Kaserne), located a few miles from Dora in the city of Nordhausen. There, lethargic inmates were thrown on straw beds mixed with excrement and left to slowly die of starvation and dehydration. Many were exhausted, emaciated Jews who had been through the ranks of concentration camps and whose last ounce of strength was spent on the transport to Camp Dora.

In February Richard Baer, the commandant of Auschwitz, relieved Commandant Otto Forschner of his post and instated a more vicious regime of terror at Camp Dora. With his focus on the Soviet Resistance, Baer began a wave of hangings in February and March. In March, three hundred executions included 133 Russians, twenty-six Poles, three Czechs, and a Lithuanian. According to Biderman, "Many of the victims were Jews, even though today they are always referred to as Poles, Russians, Hungarians, Czechs . . . they are never classified as Jews," he wrote, "yet, when they were doomed to destruction, the only reason for it was their Jewishness."

The majority of people who suffered in the Mittelbau Dora complex were French, yet many Jews also suffered and died there. The percentage of Jews who died in Dora may never be known, since (1) Jews who "disappeared" were never counted, (2) many were not recognized as Jews due to false identity papers, and (3) Jewish transports were immediately warned by fellow inmates to disguise themselves for the reason that, "Jews do not last long at Dora."

The mass hangings caused fifty-three terrified Soviet prisoners to escape from the bunker, killing a few of the guards. The inmates were later shot down and brutally murdered. Afterward, malicious hangings took place on the roll call grounds, and multiple hangings on the overhead crane inside the tunnel. As they hung, a group of emaciated Gypsy musicians transported to Dora were forced to play military marches by the tunnels. Inmates had to march to work in step with the beat. In his book, *Planet Dora*, Yves Beón describes having to work in Hall 41 beneath the bodies of twelve men who had been hung on the overhead crane:

> Most of their bodies have lost both trousers and shoes, and puddles of urine cover the floor. Since the ropes are long, the bodies swing gently about five feet above the floor, and you have to push them aside as you advance. As you make your way through, you receive bumps from knees and tibias soaked in urine, and the corpses, pushed against each other, begin to spin around ... the SS watch the changing of shifts ... they are laughing.

Transports caused overcrowding in the Mittelbau. By March the camp was filled with craftsmen and laborers from Buchenwald, Mauthausen, Dachau, Flossenburg, Auschwitz, Gross-Rosen, and others. There was not enough food to feed the nineteen thousand inmates of Dora and the forty thousand in the Mittelbau complex. To survive, inmates hid corpses to gain a bowl of soup and a piece of bread. From December 24 to March 23, camp records show 5,321 deaths within the Mittelbau complex; about 1,090 were in Dora. From January 20 to April 3, 1943, bodies were sent from Nordhausen Death Camp to the Dora crematorium.

According to Biderman, out of 165 members of his transport, only fourteen or fifteen made it to Dora alive. Those who died were never added to Dora records. Many were left to rot by their machines. They were literally worked to death with no food or water in their stomachs. Dora was so overwhelmed with bodies the crematorium couldn't keep up. They once again began sending the bodies back to Buchenwald to be burned.

During this time, Galione had lost contact with his platoon and joined a few men of another group. As they came ashore from the Rhine River, the Germans had been waiting for them and began firing shells. Shrapnel from an exploding bomb ripped into the shinbone of Galione's left leg, shattering bone. A Western Union telegram was sent to his wife Iolé saying, "The secretary of war desired me to express his deep regret that Pfc. Galione John M. was slightly wounded in Germany 24 March 1945."

Meanwhile, on April 2 at 8 a.m., the SS halted prisoners from Barracks 10, rather than sending them to their work area. Inmates watching became so frightened that some screamed, scattered, and once again tried to escape. Frail prisoners with labored breathing hid between barracks, while others endured a brutal clubbing. Thousands disappeared. A manhunt was organized. German guards warned those hiding to come out or die by clubbing. When they revealed themselves they were mercilessly clubbed. Inmates were told they would be liquidated and the camp destroyed with flamethrowers. Hitler said prisoners should "share the annihilation." Hitler wanted the SS to blow up all concentration camps with their inmates in order to cover their crimes.

As the prisoners of Dora died of starvation, disease and brutality, von Braun heard rumors that Hitler had ordered the Secret Police to liquidate the entire rocket team. He had experienced a previous scare with the Gestapo in March of 1944 when he was thrown in jail for "crimes against the state" after he spoke of building rockets for space travel instead of war. Dornberger later caused his release when he told the SS and Gestapo that Hitler would have them all shot because without von Braun there will be no V-2 weapon.

Peenemünde and Camp Dora were located in the Soviet zone of occupation. The SS had been instructed to "let no scientist be captured" by Soviet or Allied Army. Hitler planned to eliminate the rocket experts to avoid a Russian capture of their missile technology. In this light, Peenemünde with its barbed-wire fencing had now become von Braun's prison. After holding a secret meeting with his colleagues in a local farmhouse free of hidden microphones, von Braun tricked the SS guards into believing they had been ordered to leave Peenemünde. He escaped to Bleicherode with a convoy of hundreds under the bogus name, "Project for Special Dispositions."

Nonetheless, their stay in Bleicherode ended suddenly. In an effort to secure a bargaining chip presentable to the Allies, General Kammler took von Braun and five hundred key rocket scientists hostage on April 2 and placed them in an old Army camp surrounded by barbed wire fencing, near Oberammergau in southern Germany. The next day, von Braun ordered his personal aides, Bernhard Tessmann and Dieter Huzel, to hide fourteen tons of the most vital V-2 missile documents in an abandoned mine northwest of the Mittelwerk. The documents were hauled to the heart of the mine by tramcar and the roof was blown up to conceal them.

As the enemies drew near, von Braun and his team feared that SS guards might kill them for their knowledge. He persuaded an SS officer to allow the rocket specialists to disperse into smaller villages to prevent the entire team from being killed in an Allied bombing. With dispersion, there will be "some to carry on the secret weapon project." The next day the officer divided the prisoners into smaller groups and escorted them to neighboring villages. Meanwhile, Dornberger's team was evacuated on April 6. In the end, Dornberger, von Braun, and a hundred others ended up in Oberjoch Ski Lodge on the former Austrian-German border. While von Braun and his team awaited their fate, prisoners at Camp Dora faced a terrifying evacuation of their own.

On April 3, about two thousand inmates from Dora were sent to Harzungen. That same night, twelve hundred dying prisoners at the Nordhausen Death Camp were accidentally killed in an Allied bombing. Camp administration discussed blowing up Dora and its prisoners in order to eliminate evidence of all that had taken place. In the late afternoon of April 4, the SS pulled seven leading German Communists out of the bunker prison and murdered them by firing squad. Biderman, who survived the Lodz Ghetto, Auschwitz-Birkenau, Althammer and Dora, wrote: "This was the first time in a concentration camp that I had been present at an execution by firing squad."

The massive evacuations began on April 5. About thirty thousand inmates of the Mittelbau were forced into trains and shipped to Bergen-Belsen. Thousands more were taken on death marches. Those who lagged were shot and killed by the road. Others were taken on what seemed to be a never-ending train ride to impending death. During one of the train rides, a large group of French officers were lined up outside and mowed down with machine guns. Michel Depierre escaped death when he hid after seeing Nazi guards beating the evacuees with tool handles. Depierre wrote in his memoir: "I went around the block and pushed a window that thank God opened. I'm in an empty room and my heart is beating really fast. I collapse and lose consciousness."

By the age of only eighteen-years-old, George Benedict had survived the death march from Auschwitz to Buchenwald and then to Dora, but by April he was weary. Benedict describes how he escaped the evacuation: "I was in Dora when the Nazis evacuated the camp. I hid in the rafters. I did not want to endure another death march. I'd had enough experience! Dora was as bad as Auschwitz, without gas chambers."

On April 9 and 10 the SS abandoned the prisoners of Dora, locking them inside the camp with no food or water. The victims of Dora had endured starvation, dehydration, exhaustion, brutality and horror; they had seen their friends murdered, gruesomely hanged, clubbed, tortured, and mowed down with machine guns. Giving up all hope that the D-day soldiers would find them, with their last reserves of strength they dragged themselves to the infirmary to die. "It is the prisoner's 'Way of the Cross,'" wrote Beón, "and for them, it's finished."

April 10, 1945: While those in the infirmary lay waiting to die, walking skeletons in Dora wandered through the camp in a daze. Suddenly, at about 2:30 p.m. gunfire jolted the sick and weary from their hopelessness. A group of excited inmates ran to see who was getting shot. A lone American soldier was seen climbing up the hillside in an effort to take cover over top the tunnel entrance. A German guard ran after him, shooting.

Inmates rushed to stand by the guardhouse and watch the front gate, hoping the soldier would see that they were captives in need of rescue. At approximately 4:50 p.m., prisoners waiting by the gate couldn't believe their eyes as they watched the lone soldier, who was wearing a Timberwolf patch on his left shoulder, struggle to break the burly lock on the gate that held them captive.

After a five-day search on foot for the prisoners of concentration camps, Private John Michael Galione had discovered the hidden camp holding the "Mother Lode" of Germany's missile technology! How he had found the most secret camp in Germany only days after being wounded at the Rhine River is an astounding story of courage, strength, and persistence. Galione was raised to be tough and tearless, but he wept as he told his daughter, Mary, the story he had buried in his heart for fifty years.

Chapter 4

Saving the Prisoners of Dora

From October 1944 until the crossing of the Rhine River Private Galione had been shelled, shot at, nearly drowned, and almost killed by land mines; yet he somehow managed to escape injury. But after crossing the Rhine River in March of 1945, shrapnel from an exploding shell ripped into the shinbone of his left leg. With a wound on his leg, Galione advanced with his comrades 175 miles in nine days. According to Galione, all through those miles, "we were engaged in continuous battle." Exhausted and war weary, on April 4, 1945, Galione and his unit stopped to rest in the Lippstadt area. Galione shares his notable first-hand account:

> We needed to pull over and rest, but we were the American troops. We couldn't just stop without having a good reason, so we wrote it up as maintenance and we worked on our jeeps. On April 4, I and a couple of my buddies stood leaning with one foot up on a fence, just shootin' the breeze. We talked about how lucky we were to have made it that far in the war. We talked about how happy we were that we would probably make it home to our families. After all we had been through, it felt good to just rest and talk about our families. You know, until then, when we talked it was always about war. We pulled out maps, discussed strategies, and made plans. It felt good to talk about something other than war.

Suddenly, as the evening of April 4 turned to the dark early morning of April 5 Galione's feeling of camaraderie was tackled by a gut sense of doom and urgency.

It was about 3 a.m.: We smelled an odor. I said, "Hey Sarge, what do you think that odor could be? I get a *bad* feeling with it." He said there was a rumor that there might be a labor camp in the area where the Nazis are keeping prisoners. The rumor came from the Russians who had found a camp a few weeks earlier. Something was telling me that the odor had something to do with the prisoners, that they were somehow connected. I just had a *bad* feeling. I went to my sergeant and asked for permission to go in and get the people out. I wanted to go in with the three or four guys I always hung with. There were actually five of us, but three of us were always together. We watched each other's back and we had been good together in battle. We trusted each other. The sarge said, "It's too dangerous. This would not be enough men to send in, and we don't even know where the Nazis are keeping the prisoners."

I don't know what it was, but for some reason I couldn't let it go. Throughout the day I tried to forget it, but as the day wore on something kept driving me to investigate and pursue it. Something kept *nagging* me. I tried to talk to the other guys about where the Nazis might be keeping the prisoners, but they didn't want to discuss it. It's important that you understand that it wasn't because they were lazy or coward, or didn't want to help. In fact, our platoon was known as the toughest in the infantry. We had fought hard and won many battles, many victories. Some of the men in our group were already heroes. A couple of the guys in our group had done some pretty courageous things and were highly decorated for those things. But I know what it was: they were tired from war.

By April 4, we had just come in from a seventy-five mile advance and we had gone a hundred miles before that; and all through those miles we fought hard and continuously in battle. We needed to recuperate from all we had been through. We had watched so many of our friends die right in front of us. It affected us psychologically. I was standing right next to my best friend, Steve Harmanos, when he stepped on a land mine that blew up. I went through a hard time after that.

Those who were still alive by April 4 felt lucky to have made it this far in the war. Some of them had families to return home to. They were tired of taking risks. I know, because I felt the same way they did. I was tired, but something kept driving me to find the prisoners. I just had a gut feeling something horrible was going on. Only one guy would discuss it with me, and he was my good friend. So, we put our heads together.

"If only we could find out how the Nazis are bringing the prisoners in we could intercept them, hold them at gunpoint, and force them to bring us to their camp," I said. We asked ourselves, "What would be the best way for the Nazis to sneak large numbers of people through the neighborhoods and into the camp without being seen?"

THE TRAINS! We figured they must have been bringing them in on the trains! All that day, something kept nagging me, telling me to go, to follow the trains. By the end of the day, the feeling was strong. I knew I wouldn't be able to sleep that night. It was getting near time to turn in. I thought, "If I could find the camp during the night while everybody's sleeping, I could bring back this information for the sarge by morning. If I can locate the camp, then maybe he will agree to send us in to get the people out." I couldn't shake the feeling that if there were prisoners, the Germans were most likely torturing them. You see, if you were captured the Nazis didn't just keep you prisoner; they would do terrible things to you. They would torture you. We knew that because, earlier in the war, we had found a dead man who had been tortured for information in a tub of water.

Hey, if I were prisoner of the Nazis I'd want somebody to come looking for *me*. So, when all the soldiers were getting into their sleeping bags that night, I left to follow the trains. It was about nine or nine thirty at night when I left. Before I left, I told one of my buddies to let the sarge know I had gone to locate the camp. That way, in case I didn't make it back by morning he'd know I didn't just desert. He'd know I was working on a mission. I asked my buddy to go with me, but he didn't want to go, and usually he would go anywhere I'd ask.

See, I was fairly certain that we were right about the Nazis using the trains to transport the prisoners. I had planned to jump the train and intercept the Nazi guards as they transported the prisoners to the camp. I knew the Germans would use two guards at the most for this task, and I knew I could handle that by myself. I had taken several Nazis prisoner a few weeks earlier. (February 23 - Roer River) I planned to put a gun to the guard's head. Nobody wants to die. With his life at stake, I knew he would take me to the camp. Even if he had been with a partner, I knew he wouldn't want him to die. The Germans gave up easily.

I walked and walked all night. The hours passed. I was exhausted because we had just gotten in from all those miles. My legs were tired, weak, and the wound on my leg was raw. My boot kept digging in. I had to keep putting something in there to cushion the wound. When I saw that there had been no activity by the trains all night, I was beginning to think my gut feeling was wrong. I had planned to search for the prisoners while everybody was sleeping and return with information for the sarge by three or three thirty in the morning. I realized I had walked past the time that I had planned to turn around and walk back. I had intended to turn around by midnight, and it was about one or one thirty in the morning.

But when I started to think about turning around, something overpowering came over me. I don't know what it was. My legs just kept walking. It was like somebody had pushed me from behind. It was strong! I turned around to see who pushed me, but nobody was there. I thought perhaps my buddy had changed his mind and decided to come with me. I knew it wasn't a German soldier. A German soldier wouldn't have pushed me first; he would have just shot me from behind. It was like somebody had shoved me, grabbed me at the elbows, and pushed me forward. I don't even know where my energy was coming from. My legs were tired, but something was making me walk, telling me to keep following the trains; and at the same time it gave me the strength to keep going. As I walked, I wondered what kind of trouble I could be in if I didn't turn around and return by morning. But something kept telling me to keep following the trains. The feeling was so strong. I just couldn't shake it.

I walked for *days!* While I was walking, I could see from afar where American troops were camped out. I thought about going over to them, but something kept telling me not to stray, to keep walking and not stop. During the nights I followed the trains closely, hoping to jump the train and catch the Nazis transporting the prisoners. But in the day I followed the trains from up inside the woods, moving slower. That's how we had been trained. We were nightfighters. That was General Terry Allen's strategy and it helped me to survive. While I was in the woods I'd lay my head against a tree for an hour or so to get a little rest, but I never slept. There was too much German activity down by the road. It was *dangerous* territory. I was afraid if I fell asleep I'd be killed.

APRIL 10, 1945: DISCOVERING HORROR

For days I followed the trains all the way down and found a train car filled with dead bodies. The first train car was empty and it stunk. I knew I was on to something, so I kept walking and the next train car that I found was filled with dead bodies. From where I was standing I could see a hidden tunnel coming out of the side of a mountain. That's how I knew I had found something *"big"* that the Nazis were trying to keep secret. I knew there was a reason the Germans would go through the trouble of building an entrance hidden inside a mountain, and then cover it with camouflage.

I went into the tunnel to investigate. I smelled an odor inside the tunnel that led me to believe the Nazis might be making some kind of munitions, weapons inside the mountain. But I didn't want to go in too deep because I was alone. I didn't even have a jeep for escape. If I'd had a jeep I would have gone deeper, but without a vehicle I knew the Germans could surround me at both ends of the tunnel and there was nowhere to run and take cover. I would be trapped. So, I went back to investigate the bodies and to try and figure out what the Germans were doing.

The bodies didn't look like normal people look when you die. They looked like skeletons wrapped in skin, and they didn't have clothes on. By the condition of the bodies I could tell the people had only been dead about a day or two. In order to figure out what was going on, I needed to identify whether these were the bodies of Russians, Germans, or American soldiers. That's how it is in war. It's important to find out who's who so you can figure out what's going on.

While I was investigating the tunnel and the bodies, trying to find some kind of identification underneath the bodies—a patch, a uniform, anything that would tell me whether they were the bodies of Russians, Germans, or American soldiers—I was spotted by a German guard who looked like he was leaving. I had seen him before, packing supplies in boxes on top of his truck. I was trying to be quiet as I used my gun to move the bodies, to lift their arms and legs, hoping to find some kind of clue underneath the bodies that would tell me who these people were. But my legs were weak and wobbly from walking for days with no sleep. When I leaned over I lost my footing. My gun hit the side of the train car and my spare ammo clip fell off of me, hit the ground, and made a noise. If I hadn't been so tired, I would have been more careful. It would have never happened.

He heard me and came running over shooting. I took cover on top of the tunnel, around where the trains would run. This is where it would have been good to have a soldier to cover me. It was hard getting up there. I could have easily been killed. I don't know how he missed me. Bullets were flying past me on both sides. A couple of them whizzed right by my ear! We shot back and forth for a while, but he was in a hurry to get out of there. I don't think the Germans wanted to die this late in the war either. But, for a moment, I didn't think I'd make it out of there. Looking back, there must have been an angel shielding me from the bullets, keeping me alive until I found the prisoners, because it was right after that I discovered the prisoners at the gate.

From on top of the hill, I walked around the camp and I ended up at the front gate. I was standing in front of a gate that was locked with a strong lock. That's how the Nazis would do it when they kept prisoners. I had seen this before when we freed our own men. They put you behind a gate, lock you in with a strong lock, and assign a couple of guards to watch the gate. That's all. I figured this might be the camp where the Nazis were keeping the prisoners, but I needed to get inside to investigate further. I was there for a while trying to break the lock, but I didn't want to stay too long with no soldier to cover me and no jeep in which to escape.

The Heroic Journey of Private Galione

Tunnel B: The camouflaged entrance of the underground factory. (USHMM)

I had seen some of the prisoners standing there watching me from behind a building. They were just standing there, watching me. (Galione smiled because his hunch panned out. He was now standing face-to-face with the prisoners.) But because I wasn't sure who they were or what was going on—and I didn't know if there were any more German guards around—I didn't want to stay there. It was a bad spot. There was nowhere to run and take cover. On one side was a mountain and on the other side was an open field. I had already tried climbing the mountain and was almost killed. To stay there would have made me a sitting duck. If I'd had a jeep to escape with, I could have taken more chances. I could have even used the jeep to break through the gate.

I wasn't only worried about dying for myself, but now I had important information that I needed to pass on to my sergeant. In war, you have to think that way. What good would I be to the prisoners if I were shot and killed right there by the gate? Then, no one would have ever found them. The camp was in such a hidden place, and our soldiers were not in position to advance upon it. The camp was located down a secluded side road hidden along a curve in the road, so that when you look down that street from the main road you can't see it.

While I was at the gate trying to twist the lock with my gun, I remembered passing American soldiers of another group. I had seen where they were encamped. So, I decided to walk back to where they were to see if I could obtain at least a jeep, but another soldier would be better. I was going to ask for whatever they would give me.

It had been about two thirty in the afternoon when I was by the train car with the dead bodies and the German guard came running over shooting. When I found the prisoners at the gate it was closer to five o'clock. It was getting near time for the sun to start going down. During that time in April the sun was still going down early. It had taken me almost five days to get there. (Private Galione followed the trains from the evening of April 5 to early afternoon on April 10.) I hadn't had any sleep in all that time. Above the tunnel, there were thick woods. I went deep into the woods to find a safe place where I could get a couple hours rest before having to walk again. It was about five thirty when I found a spot where I thought it was safe. I was exhausted, weak.

When I woke up, the timing was perfect for me to continue walking in the dark. That way, I could travel faster and without being seen. I started to walk in the direction where I had remembered seeing the soldiers. It was a miracle. On the way, I spotted two soldiers with a jeep broke down on the side of the road. It was about 1 a.m. when I found them. They were from the 929 (a Timberwolf attachment).

I went over to one of the soldiers, looked at the jeep, and smiled. It was like a plum waiting to be picked. Looking back, I realize that God had been helping me to rescue the prisoners faster because they were on their last leg. Only, I didn't know that at this time. Here I had found the prisoners and now when I need a jeep there's one delivered to me broke down on the side of the road—and it was something so simple to fix! Finding the jeep and soldiers on the road saved me a lot of time walking. If I had to walk all the way to where I had seen the soldiers camped out, it would have taken me another day or so of walking and the people at the camp would have all died. They were in such bad shape when we later found them in the infirmary, every second counted.

I told the soldier that I had found something *"big"* that the Nazis were trying to keep secret, but that I wasn't exactly sure of what it was.[2] I told him I would fix his jeep if he'd come back with me and help me break the lock on the gate. He said he couldn't come because he had chores to do for his commander, and now he was really behind because the jeep had broken down. I told him I would help him with his chores, but explained it was of utmost urgency that he comes with me. I told him I had found a train car filled with dead bodies and that we had to find out whether they were the bodies of Russians, Germans, or American soldiers.

The soldier agreed, but first he wanted to drive back and ask his commander for permission. I fixed the jeep and we drove back to tell his commander what I had found, and to ask permission for the soldiers to come back with me and help me break the lock. But when the commander heard about what I had found—secret tunnel, dead prisoners—he wanted to go himself and he wanted to pick up another buddy of his. So, we went to pick him up.[3] He let me sit in the front and I led them to the camp.

APRIL 11, 1945: PENETRATING HELL

April 11, 1945: Private Galione brought the commander and his friend to the locked gate at Camp Dora. In the early afternoon of April 10, Galione was the first American soldier to discover Mittelbau Dora Concentration Camp and the secret tunnels. He and the soldiers he brought back to the camp to help him break the lock on April 11 were the first American soldiers to penetrate the camp and witness the unspeakable horrors within the gates.

> There were three of us that night that went to break the lock on the gate, but one sat in the jeep keeping watch. We worked on the lock just a little while and then it opened.[4] We started to drive into the camp, slowly at first, while looking around. The sun had not yet come up, but the glow of the sun was just starting to light the earth to where we could begin to see a little more of what was in the camp. (Galione's eyes opened wide as he remembered the first glow of sun bringing to light a multitude of emaciated corpses lying throughout the camp.)
>
> What we saw in there was like something out of a horror movie! There were dead bodies, but their bodies were not normal; they were gray in color and they looked like skeletons wrapped in skin. Some of them were so thin you could see their backbones through their stomachs. Then, somebody who looked like he was in a horror movie ran up to us pointing to one of the buildings and saying something like, "There are people in here." The soldier in the jeep spoke French and translated what he said.

The withered inmate led them to the infirmary where sick prisoners of Dora lay dying of starvation. "The driver was so afraid we would be captured that he didn't want to separate from the jeep, in case we might have to make a fast getaway," said Galione. "So he pulled the jeep up close to the door and with one foot inside the jeep and one foot in the building he peaked inside and jumped back into the jeep." Inside he saw the frightening sight of about one hundred living skeletons too weak to move and barely breathing. Horrified, they drove away from the infirmary and were struck by fear and terror unmatched by any they had ever faced in war as they came upon the shocking sight of a pile of twisted corpses stacked high in a corner of the camp. It was all the fright they could bear. Galione tells the story:

> We came to a point where we were approaching a corner and would have to turn the jeep around. We were so frightened by what we saw in there that we put the jeep in reverse and drove out backwards real fast! The soldier driving the jeep didn't even want to take the time to turn the jeep around until we got out of there, to where the road was. That's how frightened we were that we might be captured. We just wanted to get out of there. We didn't know *what* was going on in there and we didn't want to end up like the people we saw. The German guards had abandoned the prisoners, but we didn't know that at the time. To be safe we wanted to bring in more men.

THE DECISION TO RESCUE

> I didn't have to walk all the way back. The soldiers from the 929 drove me back to my sergeant. It took us about two and a half to two and three quarter hours to drive back by jeep. That means I had walked over a hundred miles while I was searching for the camp. The distance I walked was like walking from my house in Bristol, Pennsylvania, to Atlantic City, New Jersey, and part of the way back.
>
> I told the sergeant I had located a camp. I told him all about what I had found: the bodies, the prisoners, everything. He didn't want to go because the German guard had seen me they would know we were coming. He was afraid our whole platoon could be killed in an ambush. You see, when the Germans knew the Americans were coming, that's what they would do; they would set up an ambush. Whole groups of men had died this way. I understood his concern, but we couldn't just decide not to go.
>
> "We *HAVE* to go!" I said. "We'll go in from another direction,

but we *have* to go! The people who are still alive in the camp are in bad shape. They're barely breathing. They have one or two respirations per minute. They're on their last leg. They might only have a day or two left to live. I found a train car filled with dead people that stink to high heaven and they don't have uniforms on. We have to find out who these people are. For all we know, they could be our own American boys!"

"I was thrilled!" said Galione. "The next day they sent us in to rescue the people. I couldn't believe it. They sent in a whole gang of us! They pulled men from different areas: tanks, medical teams, the Red Cross, the 414th. . . . I was so happy. I couldn't have asked for anything better!"

On April 11, 1945, Sergeant Puryear agreed to the rescue, yet ordered Galione never to reveal that he had saved the prisoners. Galione believed his story was silenced when the sarge realized that if he had given him permission to scout he would have received a jeep, backup, and reached Dora a week earlier, saving more lives. Sadly, Puryear held himself responsible for a tragedy he could not have foreseen. Even so, when Galione's trek to Dora was buried, the survivors were deprived of knowing the story of their rescue, the world was kept from learning a true and important history, and the troops he directed to Camp Dora were recognized, while Galione remained unknown. Still, Galione's discovery and Puryear's decision to go in and rescue worked together to save the remnant of prisoners in Dora and related camps. "I didn't care about getting the credit," said Galione. "I was just so happy we were going in to rescue. The people were in such bad shape. I don't think they had another day left to live."

GALIONE RADIOES THE TROOPS

The sarge asked me to radio the Third Armored Division to give them directions to Camp Dora.[5] See, the Third Armored would support us at various times in the war. They were closer to the camp than we were, and they would be coming in from another direction. This was good, because the main reason we called in the Third Armored was to protect us from ambush. Since the German guard had seen me, they would know we were coming. Our plan was to send the Third Armored to the camp first, before we, the Timberwolves, arrive. That way they could take care of any Germans who might have set up an ambush for us.[6] It was important that we wait until they get there first.

I radioed Combat B of the Third Armored about eleven thirty in the morning. I called Taskforce Lovelady. Taskforce Lovelady and Taskforce Wellborn were both under Combat Command Boudinot. I radioed the 104th attachments too. The sarge called the medical teams. I believe he called Colonel Taggart.[7] I told the Third Armored about the camp and the prisoners, but I was so exhausted from the whole ordeal; I didn't go into detail about the hidden tunnel. I just told them to "divert" to the Nordhausen area where they would find "something unique" that the Germans had done, where "something strange" was going on.[8] I figured if they followed my directions they would find it. But when I gave the Third Armored directions to Camp Dora, I failed to consider the direction they would be coming from. After all, I didn't take the road; I traveled through the woods. I was tired and forgot to tell them about the curve in the road.[9] But this was meant to be because it caused a miracle.

APRIL 12: GALIONE LEADS TASKFORCE KELLEHER TO CAMP MITTELBAU DORA

Early the next morning Taskforce Kelleher pulled up to our encampment.[10] See, they were of the 414th and I was of the 415th. We were all of the same Infantry Division, but of a different Regiment. They came in the middle of the night, while it was still dark. The sarge asked me to lead them to the camp, because

I had found the camp and would know how to get there from where we were. He didn't want to take a chance of the 414th getting lost. Because it was near the end of the war, he didn't want to be responsible for anything bad that might happen to them. Also, time had passed. The people in the camp didn't have long to live. I was glad he asked me to go.

On the way to the camp, the soldiers from the 414th were asking me questions; they wanted to know who found the camp. They were amazed, wanting to know how in the world any of our soldiers were able to find this camp, since it was located in such an out-of-the-way place and it wasn't along the course we were traveling. But I obeyed the order; I didn't tell them it was me.

The Third Armored was supposed to beat us to the camp in order to protect us from ambush, but when we got to the camp we wondered where the Third Armored was. They were nowhere in sight. We didn't understand what had happened. We had gotten a call saying it was OK to go in. It was dangerous for us to be there without support, but we still worked, staying alert and looking around. Camp Dora was in *extreme* enemy territory. One of the first things we did was set up shop in the basement of an abandoned house. We wanted to make sure we had a safe place to sleep during the time we would be staying there and working at the camp. We didn't want to sleep in tents, because we could be easily bombed. There's no protection. In a basement we would be safe from bombing.

At the camp, one of the prisoners thought that somebody might still be alive in one of the bunkers, but we couldn't break the lock. We went back to the house to gather supplies and to search for a special tool. We planned to go across the street to a house where a German man lived. We were going to see if he had a special tool that we could use to break the lock on the bunker.

But when the German man looked out his window and saw three American soldiers pointing and coming toward his house, he thought we were coming to kill him, so he hung himself in the garage. *That's* how bad it was back then. He would rather die by his own hand than by the bullet of an American soldier.

THE MIRACLE IN GETTING LOST

While we were working at the camp we waited to hear what had happened to the Third Armored Division. Hours later we received word from a guy who came back to tell us that the Third Armored had gotten lost in the tunnels and ended up at another camp by accident. But this was meant to be. As they went down the road following my directions they missed Camp Dora all together. Instead, they got lost in the tunnels and found about four hundred and fifty, possibly five hundred, more dying prisoners at a second camp a few miles from Dora called, Camp Nordhausen. The real name of that camp was Boelcke-Kaserne. The 555th Timberwolf attachment also found that camp. They drove their jeeps right over the barbed wire fencing. A captain named Bill Warmington was the first to break through the fence. I was glad to hear the 555th had found the other camp, because it meant that our division (the 104th) was involved in liberating the entire Mittelbau complex.[11]

THE TROOPS ARRIVE

Private Galione's five-day search for the prisoners of concentration camps resulted in various attachments of the First Army turning from their course to Halle and Berlin, and diverting in a caravan of trucks to the Nordhausen area. Some of them were from the 329th Medical Battalion, the 750th Tank Battalion, the 387th Field Artillery Battalion, the 414th Infantry Regiment, the 415th Infantry Regiment, the 929th Field Artillery Battalion, the 555th Anti-Aircraft Automatic Weapons Battalion, the Third Armored Division, the VII Corp, the Red Cross, and others. Most of the attachments sent in were members of the 104th Timberwolf Army Infantry Division and Third Armored Division. Galione helped liberate both Dora and Nordhausen and filmed the atrocities.

"That camp was even worse than the one I found," said Galione. "There were children in there. They found the bones of babies and very small children that had been burned. There were women with their breasts cut off; men hung by their scrotum. It was so horrible; I don't even want to go into it."

Captain Warmington's handwritten account states, "The torture chambers were covered with the imprints of feet, which had kicked and kicked before death had finally come." One of the liberators who witnessed the unspeakable horrors at Nordhausen Death Camp was Tech. Sergeant Harold Bruce Welch, father of First Lady Laura Bush. Prisoners at this camp had been starved and tortured, and they endured an accidental Allied bombing the week before they were found. Sergeant Ragene Farris of the 329th Medical Battalion of the 104th Infantry Division was given the enormous task of coordinating the rescue effort. "Bombs had ground flesh and bones into the cement floor," Farris wrote in his memoir. Others found lying in wooden beds on a second floor were "grotesquely still, yet hanging tenaciously to life's breath. *They were still alive!*"

At Camp Dora Private Galione and the Special Task Force worked as they waited for the troops to arrive. Sergeant Puryear described the story to Galione's daughter, Mary: "We went in trucks a good distance and pulled into the camp at three fifteen in the afternoon," said Sergeant Puryear. "Camp Dora was located on the right-hand side of the road, right in the curve of the road. It must have been an angel who sent your father to find the prisoners, because when we arrived they were stacked like cordwood, waiting to die." Galione describes the reaction of his comrades upon entering the gate:

The Heroic Journey of Private Galione

Two survivors lay amongst many corpses at Boelcke-Kaserne, more commonly known as Nordhausen Death Camp (USHMM-83409)

We thought nothing could hurt us. We were hard from war. But when we walked in there, we couldn't help getting choked up. I had been there before, so I knew what to expect. But some of the soldiers cried and some of them got sick to their stomachs. You know, they turned aside and threw up by the fence. There were dead bodies piled up. The smell was so bad, like nothing you can imagine. We couldn't believe any human being could be so cruel.

"Some of the bodies were lying in open trenches, some were stacked in buildings, and others were piled out in the open," wrote Nelson C. Eaton in his memoir. "Most of them, you could see their spinal columns thru their stomach muscles, and their appendages were nothing but skin and bones." In a letter dated April 4, 2000, Blaine Passey, 1st Lt. and Captain in the Medical Administrative Corp., whose unit was responsible for evacuating the wounded of the First Army from the front lines, describes what he saw at Camp Dora:

Saving the Prisoners of Dora

Standing with camera in hand, Private Galione filmed the Dora-Nordhausen complex, the atrocities, and the secret underground factory. Having walked five days searching for prisoners, and then to find them in such horror, explains why his expression is one of anger and exhaustion.

> The horrors of the concentration camp at Dora, a few miles north of Nordhausen, were so great that most men experiencing it would try to forget them . . . what we saw there was indescribable. Most of the bodies of prisoners were piled high in a corner of the camp. In later pictures of them, they were all laid out in rows awaiting burial. The barracks revealed scenes just as bad or worse. Bodies were lying on shelves two feet by two feet, stacked four shelves high. Some prisoners were living and some were dead. It was very hard to tell the difference between them, proving that all had been starved while kept there.

Inmates wept as they reached for the hands of their liberators. The scene was so heart-rending that battle-hardened men of the 104th wept too. Now, fifty years later, Galione wept as he described the emotional response of those still alive in Dora.

> The people were so happy to see us. They were tugging our clothes, feeling our uniforms between their fingers like they were gold. They just wanted to touch us. They were thanking us, hugging us; some of them were even putting their hands together and thanking God over and over again. They were so happy to see us. I imagine we were an answer to their prayers.

Suddenly, Galione burst into tears. As he struggled to release his deepest pain, the torment Mary had worked years to uncover, his throat became so thick with agony that he stretched his neck up high and bit his top lip with his bottom teeth to fight the lump in his throat and prevent deep sobbing; yet the tears streamed down his face as fifty years of bottled anguish flowed like a river.

> They looked like the walking dead. They were skin and bones. That's all. No meat. Their faces were sunken like skeletons. They were so weak we had to carry them out. Some of them were so weak they didn't even get to see their own rescue, their own

liberation. They died before getting out the gate. If only I had known the shape they were in, maybe there was something I could have done differently to get there earlier. If I had known, I wouldn't have rested; I would have kept walking. Maybe I should have pushed harder to convince the sarge to let me go. With permission I would have been given a jeep. With a jeep I would have gotten there days earlier. Many more people would have been saved. If only I had known.

Through the years that Mary sat by her father's side listening to the stories of his life, she rarely spoke. She mostly listened and let him get the war off his chest. This time, seeing him so broken caused her to step out of character. With tears, Mary laid her hand on top of his hand and with courage spoke softly to console him:

No, Dad. Don't you see? The reason God sent you to follow the trains is because the sergeant would not have given you permission to scout for prisoners. It was the end of the war. The men were exhausted and tired of taking risks. You said so yourself. Think about it. He not only urged you to follow the trains, but He sent an angel to keep you from turning around and going back. What you did to find the prisoners was tremendous. You walked for days with a wound on your leg when no one else in your unit had the strength to go. You could have rested with your comrades, but you forfeited your sleep to search for prisoners. You did everything possible to find them when no one in the infantry knew they existed. No, Dad. You had no way of knowing the prisoners were near death. You did everything the way you were supposed to. Don't you see? He instructed you to "follow the trains" because He knew there were dying people praying for rescue at the other end of the tracks. You did the right thing, Dad. You obeyed God and it brought in the troops and saved hundreds of people who would have otherwise died.

Galione pulled a hanky out of his pocket and wiped the tears from his face. "Yeah, maybe you're right," he said so solemnly. "Maybe everything that happened was the best it could be." Mary had never seen her father in such agony. "If Dad is in this much pain over only *seeing* how badly the prisoners of Dora were treated," she thought, "imagine the pain of those who actually *lived* the hellish nightmare *every day*." It is no wonder the prisoners were overjoyed to see the faces of their liberators. Still, the inmates had been starved too long. The Timberwolves had to move fast to save lives.

GALIONE PROVIDES MEAT FOR SOUP

We had to get food into them right away. I felt so sorry for the way the people had been treated. When we kids were sick my mother always made us homemade chicken soup, but there were hundreds of starving people. We would need too many chickens to get enough meat to feed them and it would take too long to prepare that many chickens. Cows would have taken too long to slaughter and butcher. So, I ran to a nearby farm that I remembered passing when I was looking for the camp. I remembered seeing two pigs behind a fence. I chose the pigs because they would be the fastest and easiest to slaughter for the most amount of meat.[12]

There was a wealthy German woman sitting up on her horse. I let her know I wanted to kill the two pigs that were behind her. I pointed at them with my gun. She refused in German. I pointed my gun at her horse, letting her know that I would kill the horse if she didn't let me have those pigs. Speaking in German, I told her to do it *"NOW! Raus! Schnell!"* You do what you have to do in war. I was prepared to take her out if I had to. She was one life, but hundreds were dying at the camp.

She only spoke German, but she understood my gun. We butchered them right there in her kitchen, with my gun on the counter by the sink. I had other weapons hanging off my body. I knew she wouldn't make trouble with a fully armed soldier. I wrapped up the meat and took the bread off her table. I packed some fresh potatoes and whatever food I could carry on my back and we made a soup for them because they were too weak to eat. We had seen a cauldron next to some black, rotten potatoes. We realized the Nazis had been feeding those potatoes to the prisoners.

The meat was so heavy I could hardly carry it back to the camp. I had to walk through *extreme* enemy territory with meat on my back that was slowing me down. I could have easily been shot and killed. I prayed all the way that I would make it back to the camp alive. Again, I thought about my father and how he used to carry a bushel of tomatoes on each shoulder and walk miles to the markets. I was never able to carry the second bushel. I never had the strength of my father, but I said to myself "If he could do it, I could do it" and I made it back to the camp. I gave the meat to the medics and we made a thin soup for them. "The Nazis are the cruelest people that ever lived," I thought. "After seeing what they did to these people, you know there is a devil!"

Sadly, the prisoners of the Mittelbau Dora complex were so hungry for food that when they saw the soup some of them went wild and gorged themselves. "I have never before seen the look in the eyes of these men as they came up for coffee and soup," said Farris. Their bodies had not seen food for so long that their digestive systems could not recognize and digest food. Many became sick with cramps; some died.

Immediately after liberation, surrounded by the corpses of fellow prisoners, survivors of Dora-Mittelbau eat. (USHMM-74808 and GSMD 711.12.03)

More people died making V-2 rockets than those at whom the rockets were fired. Camp records state that over sixty thousand people had gone through Dora, with twenty-five thousand never making it out alive. Yet, considering the thousands who were excluded from camp records, it is impossible to know exactly how many people perished.

One hundred corpses were burned daily in Dora's crematorium; the overload was sent to Buchenwald to be burned. In fact, the dead prisoners Private Galione had found in the train car on April 10 were slated for the Buchenwald crematorium. Sadly, as the liberators cared for the living and buried the dead, a large group of Dora evacuees faced unparalleled horror on April 13 in the town of Gardelegen, when the Nazis chased them into a barn, poured gasoline, and set it on fire. Words cannot express the horror they experienced before death.

Meanwhile, with the total of both camps having about 1,200 survivors needing prompt medical attention, and more than five thousand corpses needing burial, the liberating troops realized they couldn't handle the task alone. They informed the mayor of Nordhausen of his responsibility to clean up the dreadful situation in the Dora complex. The mayor told them to gather German citizens to bury the dead. Under the leadership of Colonel Jones and Chaplain Steinbeck, who spoke German, the soldiers rounded up German citizens at gunpoint, rushed them to the camp, and ordered them to bury the dead.

"The order was, *'You will work!'*" Galione said in a deep, commanding voice. Mass graves were dug on a prominent hill near the camp. The corpses were carried through the town to the graves. "The people who lived near the camp said they didn't know what was going on, but they had to know," said Galione. "I guess they figured there was nothing they could do to stop it without risking their own lives."

Saving the Prisoners of Dora

American soldiers walk past rows of corpses awaiting burial at Nordhausen Death Camp, which were removed from the barracks to their left. (USHMM-04544)

Under guard, German civilians from the town of Nordhausen dig mass graves. (USHMM-83810. Courtesy of Nancy and Michael Krzyzanowski)

Red Cross ambulances rushed about three hundred of the sick and weary to a nearby German hospital. "One of the prisoners had a badly broken arm," said Galione. "The German doctors didn't care. One of our guys had to holler at the doctors to get them to come over and give care." As for the thousands of prisoners who died, there were so many corpses in the Mittelbau complex it took days to bury them.

"When it was all over," Galione said solemnly, "I and a handful of soldiers stood over their graves crying. We did that to give them a moment of honor, because we felt so sorry for the way they had died."

According to Galione and Dora historian Gretchen Schafft, Buchenwald was found as a result of discovering Dora, because the prisoners of Dora were from Buchenwald. As a result of Private Galione's discovery of Camp Dora, 700 remaining prisoners were rescued from Camp Dora, 500 from Nordhausen Death Camp, 21,000 from Buchenwald, and von Braun's one million square foot clandestine V-2 ballistic missile operation was busted wide open—*found completely intact!* One eyewitness wrote in his memoir: "A number of huge rockets, completed except for warheads, lay on jigs where they had been constructed." Then, a platoon of the 83rd Armored Reconnaissance Battalion (a Third Armored attachment led by Lt. Duane Doherty) located the Junkers aircraft factory at Kleinbodungen. Dr. Albin Sawatzki was found in the tunnels and apprehended on April 13 by Captain Julian's 104th CIC detachment.

The American Army learned that prisoners working on an experimental V-3 missile were murdered to preserve the secrecy of the project. Immediately, United States' Army Intelligence realized the importance of the ballistic missile and the secret factory at Camp Dora. When Private Galione left his encampment to search for prisoners on April 5, he never dreamed his scouting mission would change world history and make such an impact on the United States of America.

Saving the Prisoners of Dora

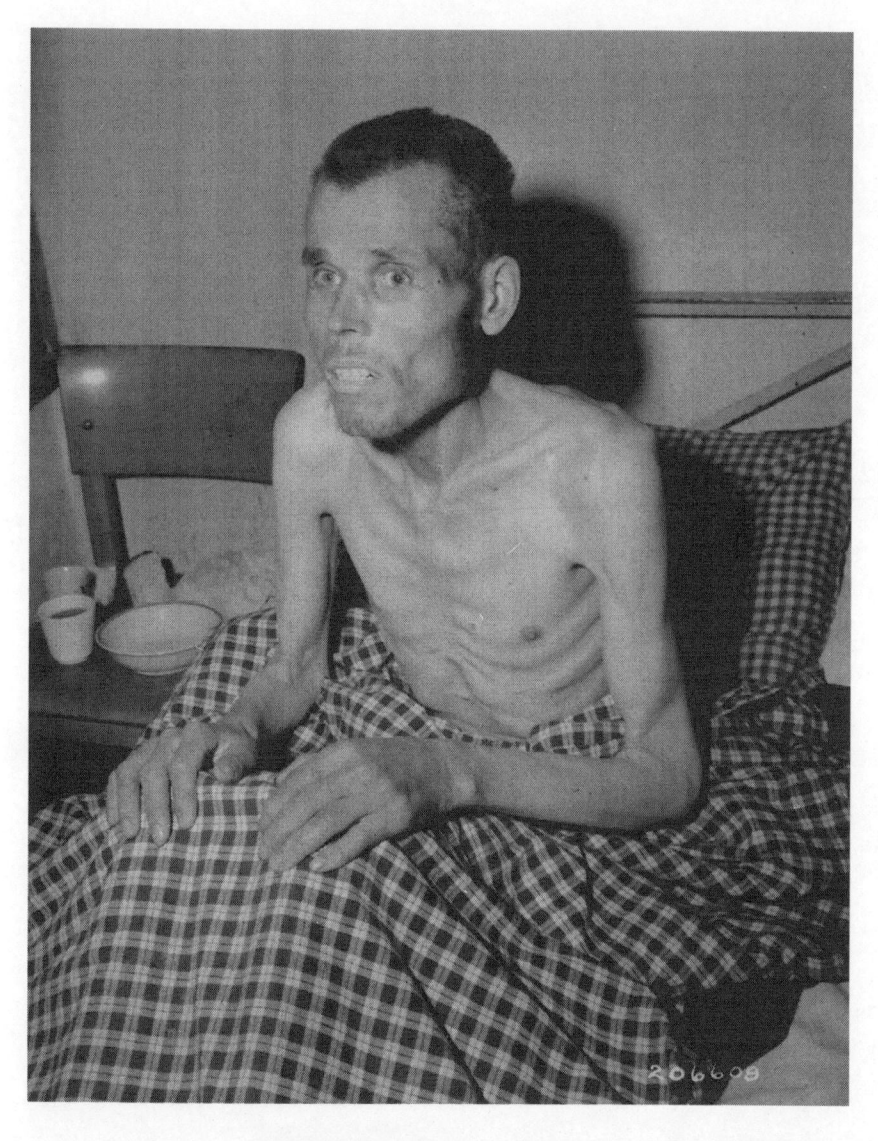

An emaciated survivor receives food and care shortly after liberation.
(GSMD and NARA III-SC-206608)

The Heroic Journey of Private Galione

American soldiers removed the outer shell of this V-2 in order to inspect the inner-workings of the ballistic missile (Peter Woodcock and Norman Yates)

V-1 Cruise Missiles found sitting on the assembly line
(Peter Woodcock and Norman Yates)

Chapter 5

The American Capture of Missile Technology

After Private Galione's search for prisoners exposed the world's first ballistic missile being secretly assembled in the largest underground factory in the world—all located in the Soviet zone of occupation—Colonel Trichel of the Pentagon's rocket department came to the sobering realization that the technological leap the Germans had made in missile development could be dangerous to the world and to the United States, especially in the hands of the Russians.

Colonel Trichel instructed the head of Technical Intelligence in Paris, Colonel Holger Toftoy, to confiscate one hundred V-2 missiles and ship them to White Sands Proving Ground in New Mexico where the Americans could analyze them. Colonel Toftoy then implemented Special Mission V-2. Major James Hamill gathered military teams to film the secret underground operation and to confiscate enough V-2 rocket parts to assemble one hundred missiles. He had been ordered to seize the rockets "without making it obvious that we had looted the place."

Meanwhile, Colonel Trichel ordered Major Robert Staver of rocket research and development to coordinate the effort to find and interrogate the German rocket experts who created the missile. Upon Staver's arrival at Nordhausen, he instructed General Electric engineers Richard Porter and Ed Hull to find and catalog German rocket technology and personnel. But, after von Braun received word that the Americans had found Camp Dora and were packing his missiles for shipment to the United States, von Braun and his associates decided to surrender to the American Army. From his red toy wagon to the supersonic missile, von Braun had worked too hard his entire life developing the rocket to consider abandoning the final product.

Despite propaganda interviews in which the Germans claimed they had planned to surrender to the Americans all along, Galione and others believed von Braun made the decision to surrender to the United States only *after* the discovery of Camp Dora and the U.S. capture of his missile operation. Had von Braun intended to surrender to the United States, he would have sought out the Americans when he fled from Peenemünde. Michael Neufeld, curator of Washington's National Air and Space Museum, mentions similar observations in his book, *The Rocket and the Reich*.

In a book read and approved by von Braun entitled, *Wernher von Braun: Rocket Engineer,* the author states that von Braun had his aides hide fourteen tons of documents in the secret tunnel "until the Third Reich rise again." This statement reveals that von Braun's true intentions were to hide until the end of the war, then restart the rocket program in Germany. The vote to surrender to the American Army was unanimous only *after* the American capture of Camp Dora and Hitler's suicide. With Hitler gone, Germany in ruins, and the missiles headed for America, the choice was clear for von Braun to follow his life's work.

On May 2, von Braun sent his brother, Magnus, bicycling down the mountain to surrender to the American Army. Magnus found Pfc. Fred Schneiker of the 324th Anti-Tank Company and explained that he was one of many German missile scientists seeking to surrender to the United States.

The American Capture of Missile Technology

The American capture of top German scientists. Center four: Major General Walter Dornberger, Lt. Col. Herbert Axter, Wernher von Braun who broke his arm in a car accident during flight, and Hans Lindenberg after surrendering to the United States' troops. Austria, May 3, 1945. (NARA, War & Conflict 1294)

After Germany surrendered on May 7, missile scientists and engineers were transported to the Bavarian ski resort of Garmisch-Partenkirchen and interrogated by British and American Intelligence teams. Doctors Fritz Zwicky, Clark Millikan, and Richard Porter questioned von Braun. On May 12, Major Staver met Karl Otto Fleisher, a V-2 engineer who referred Staver to other scientists separate from von Braun's inner circle. On May 14, Staver found the head of the rocket motor department, Walter Reidel. Reidel was interrogated through May 18. During the interrogation, he stressed using the V-2 rocket for space travel and suggested the United States transport forty of the most important V-2 engineers to America. When Colonel Toftoy realized how advanced the Germans were in missile technology, he called Washington recommending that three hundred top scientists transfer to the United States.

Meanwhile, Peenemünde, Mittelbau Dora, and the ballistic missiles were sitting in the Soviet zone of occupation. The location in which the documents were hidden would soon belong to the British. The Americans moved swiftly to confiscate the rockets and the scientific documents. On May 18, the 144th Motor Vehicle Assembly Company joined the 319th Ordnance Battalion at Camp Dora's Mittelwerk factory and began moving V-2 rocket parts out of the tunnels and loading them onto train cars. On May 22, the first forty train cars filled with rocket parts were shipped. Within nine days the last of 341 train cars left Dora-Nordhausen for Erfurt, then Antwerp, then White Sands Proving Ground, New Mexico. According to the written testimony of Lt. Col. William L. Howard, "One hundred complete V-2s were evacuated only hours before the Russians occupied the area."

Pentagon officials knew that obtaining the missiles would increase the knowledge of the American Army, but without the secret documents the Americans would be forced to engage in "reverse engineering" to decode the technology. Fleisher was the only remaining scientist in the area who knew the location of the hidden cache of secret missile documents. Major Staver tricked Fleisher into believing that von Braun had authorized him to divulge their hiding place. On May 20, Fleisher revealed the tunnel!

On May 27, "with a few hours to spare" the American Army had beaten the British to the secret documents. Three Opel trucks hauled from the mine fourteen tons of ballistic missile research labeled *"Geheim"* (German for "secret"). The documents were shipped to Paris, then to Aberdeen Proving Ground, MD. As the British objected to the captured documents, sixteen Liberty ships carrying the parts for one hundred V-2 missiles sailed from Antwerp to New Orleans and then to White Sands Proving Ground.

Sections of V-2 rockest are removed from Camp Dora by rail after the liberation, and are on their way to the United States. (USHMM-01275)

The Russian occupation of Dora was scheduled for June 21. Major Staver worked fast to procure the scientists who developed the ballistic missile. On June 8, Mittelbau engineers helped Staver identify which of the thousands of German technicians and their families should transfer to the American zone. Less than twenty-four hours before the Russians arrived, about one thousand German V-2 personnel and their families were placed aboard a fifty-car train and sent to Witzenhausen, just inside the American zone.

After preliminary interrogation and background investigations by American Intelligence Agencies, on June 20 under the code name of Operation Paperclip the United States' secretary of state, Cordell Hull, approved the transfer of about 150 of von Braun's top rocket scientists and engineers. (The mission was first dubbed Operation Overcast, and then renamed Operation Paperclip since the paperwork of those selected to transfer to the United States was marked by paperclips.) Those selected for transfer were closely guarded from the Russians and offered five-year contracts to move to the United States and work for the Army.

Meanwhile, the Soviets had gathered extensive intelligence on all ballistic missile sites and personnel. After the war, they were eager to procure von Braun and his team. But when the Soviets arrived to occupy Peenemünde and the Mittelwerk on July 5, there were no German scientists left to snatch, no rockets to confiscate and study, and very little equipment left to salvage. Private Galione's persistent gut feeling to "follow the trains and not stray" paid off, as the last rocket parts shipped out only hours before the Russians arrived. The Americans had gotten everything!

Stalin was livid! The United States had obtained the main rocket scientists, fourteen tons of secret documents on the development of the first ballistic missile, and all the V-2 rockets. By July of 1945, von Braun and other German scientists were planning their move to the United States. The United States War Department memo entitled "Outstanding German Scientists Being Brought To U.S." states: "The Secretary of War has approved a project whereby certain outstanding German scientists and technicians are being brought to this country to ensure that we take full advantage of those significant developments, which are deemed vital to our national security."

In September of 1945, the first German scientists and their families arrived in the United States at New Castle Army Air Base, south of Wilmington, Delaware. Major Hamill guarded and protected von Braun on a twenty-four-hour basis. The scientists were later flown to Boston, and then taken by boat to an Army Intelligence service post at Fort Strong in Boston Harbor. Others were transferred to Aberdeen Proving Ground, where they sorted and translated the secret documents under guard. Lieutenant Colonel Howard wrote in his account, "It is impossible to estimate the amount of time and money saved by having these scientists and technicians available to assist us in segregating, cataloging, evaluating and translating more than fourteen tons of documents."

Von Braun and 126 Peenemünders transferred to a large Army installation located at Fort Bliss, Texas, forty-seven miles south of White Sands Proving Ground. Since the Germans were several years ahead of the Americans in technology their job was to educate military, industrial, and university personnel on the intricacies of rockets and guided missiles. Their presence in America was so secret that German prisoners of war cooked for them as they settled into an abandoned hospital.

As more Germans arrived, trains delivered carloads of rocket parts from Camp Dora to White Sands Proving Ground, which were piled in the desert near Las Cruces. Von Braun and his team eventually transferred to White Sands to begin reassembling and launching V-2 rockets. By February 1946, von Braun's entire Peenemünde team had been reunited at White Sands; and on April 16 the first rebuilt V-2 was launched in the United States. The first successful launch occurred on June 28, 1946. Over time, the U.S. capture of German missile technology led to one of the most intense international competitions in history.

The Heroic Journey of Private Galione

The German Rocket Team: Under Operation Paperclip Wernher von Braun and 126 top rocket experts transferred to America to develop high-tech missiles for the United States Army at White Sands Proving Ground (NASA-MSFC-8915531)

A United States captured V-2 rocket is launched at White Sands Proving Ground (Civil Air Patrol)

THE ARMS AND SPACE RACE

Although the Americans had confiscated all the V-2 missiles, the top German scientists and the secret documents, the Russians aggressively utilized the little they had found to achieve remarkable results. By October 1946, Soviet Army Colonel, Sergei Korolyov, had Camp Dora's factory moved to the Soviet Union. Peenemünde's Helmut Gröttrup was seized and placed in charge of rebuilding the V-2 production line. On October 22, the remaining German scientists and 6,200 specialists were brought to Russia at gunpoint and made to educate Russian engineers on the intricacies of the V-2 missile.

Meanwhile, after the war Americans wanted to forget weapons and war, but von Braun warned Washington that the Russians would be working day and night using the knowledge they had gained to "strip the United States of her prestige." While von Braun launched dozens of reassembled V-2 rockets at White Sands Proving Ground, the Russians had begun launching their own V-2 rockets in October of 1947.

Von Braun informed Washington that in order to beat the Russians he'd need a testing ground having the same qualities that helped the rocket team excel at Peenemünde. A Pentagon committee suggested Cape Canaveral in Florida. Like Peenemünde, Cape Canaveral was along the ocean and had a string of island stations that could be used to track the trajectory of the rockets in flight. By 1949 the Joint Long Range Proving Ground was established there. Becker and Dornberger's "under one roof" strategy was reinstated in April of 1950 when von Braun and four hundred others of the White Sands and Fort Bliss rocket team transferred to Redstone Arsenal's Army Ballistic Missile Agency (ABMA) in Huntsville, Alabama, to develop rockets for war and space flight.

Up to 1952, sixty-four V-2 rockets were test-launched and studied at White Sands. Between 1952 and 1954, von Braun developed one of the first comprehensive space exploration programs. At Redstone, the United States' first *Intercontinental Ballistic Missile* (ICBM) was developed. The V-2 rocket was modified and became the *Redstone Rocket*. In 1955 von Braun began working with Professor Oberth on Satellite studies. In an effort to place the world's first satellite into orbit, a modified Redstone Rocket became the *Jupiter-C* rocket. While von Braun struggled to gain permission to go ahead with the project, on October 4, 1957, the Russians launched their modified V-2 rocket, the *R-7* ICBM, *Sputnik!* The Russians had succeeded in placing the world's first satellite into orbit. One month later *Sputnik-II* was launched with a passenger (a dog named Laika).

Americans who were sure of their superiority over Soviet technology were now shocked and frightened. If Soviet rockets could reach space, they could certainly reach America with an attached warhead. In response to Sputnik, von Braun launched the American-designed *Vanguard*, which burst into flames. Then on January 31, 1958, his modified Jupiter-C rocket, the *Juno-1*, launched from Cape Canaveral and placed the first American satellite into orbit, *Explorer-I*, which stayed in orbit for twelve years.

Sputnik and Explorer-I raised the intensity of the Russian-American race, becoming an all-out "Space Race." In an effort to organize space research and flights, President Eisenhower established the National Aeronautics Space Administration (NASA) on July 29, 1958. One day later, the fiftieth Redstone Rocket was launched from Johnson Island in the South Pacific. The successful Redstone launches led to the October 7 initiation of the United States' first manned space program, Project Mercury.

After Project Mercury was established, in January of 1959 the Soviets launched *Luna I*. It missed the moon, but became the first spacecraft to enter solar orbit. After Luna I, in July of the next year NASA opened the Marshall Space Flight Center (MSFC) in Huntsville, Alabama. With von Braun as director of the space center, he and his team at ABMA transferred to NASA to become the nucleus of the MSFC team. In response to Project Mercury, on April 12, 1961, the Russian *Vostok* program boosted the first man, Yuri Gagarin, into space. Three weeks later, Vostok prompted an American response, a sub-orbital flight that made Alan Shepard the first American in space.

Sputnik and Gagarin's flight drove President Kennedy to make a plea on May 25: "I believe that this nation should commit itself to achieving the goal, before this decade is out, of landing a man on the Moon and returning him safely to the Earth." Three weeks later, Russia scoffed by sending the first woman, Valentina Tereshkova, into space. Tereshkova's time in space placed the Russians far ahead of the Americans in this part of the space race. In January of 1962, America's Project Gemini was announced. The Gemini program achieved the development of crucial rendezvous techniques in space, the Ed White space walk, and first to dock with another spacecraft.

Meanwhile, in February of 1962 John Glenn became the first American man in orbit. By December, the United States' *Mariner 2* spacecraft swept past Venus. Then, the Soviet *Zond* series of spacecrafts launched in November of 1964 and July of 1965. Both achieved two flights and passed Mars. Zond intended to put a cosmonaut on the moon, but failed. To beat Gemini, in 1964 the Russians canceled Vostok and initiated the *Voskhod* program. The Americans initiated Project Pegasus.

The Voskhod program placed the Soviets farther in technology than the Americans. It was the first spacecraft capable of carrying more than one space traveler. It achieved first docking in space and the first space walk. However, as the space race intensified, haste led to two dangerous missions and the deaths of American astronauts Virgil Grissom, Edward White, and Roger Chaffee when the *Apollo I* burst into flames. Likewise, the Russian *Soyuz* program planned to send a cosmonaut to the moon and failed. In April of 1967 Vladimir Komarov came crashing down to Earth after completing seven orbits when his parachute became entangled. Komarov was the first space fatality.

In January of 1968 *Soyuz IV* and *V* docked in Earth orbit. After three more launches in October of 1969, the Soviets achieved "most cosmonauts" in orbit at one time. America sent six; Russia sent seven. Sergei Korolyov (Soviet Colonel who transferred Camp Dora's equipment to the Soviet Union) became the chief designer of Russian spacecraft after the war. He was responsible for building the *Vostok, Voshkod,* and *Soyuz*. Basically, the space race was an intense, personal competition between von Braun and Korolyov.

When President Kennedy challenged America to put the first man on the moon, von Braun was given the task of creating the massive rocket capable of thrusting him there. Under the Apollo program the *Saturn I*, the *Saturn IB*, and the *Saturn V* were developed. Arthur Rudolph, who was project director at Camp Dora, was also project director of the Saturn series. Meanwhile, the Russians had developed a giant rocket of their own, the *N-1*. Working feverishly to beat America to the moon, on February 21, 1969, the Russians launched the N-1, but it exploded in the air. Five months later the second N-1 exploded.

Finally, after twenty-three years the arms and space race came to an abrupt end. Using data collected during Gemini and the Surveyor lunar probes, on July 16, 1969, the *Saturn-V* rocket shot the *Apollo-11* spacecraft with Neal Armstrong, Buzz Aldrin, and Michael Collins to the moon! Although the United States trailed behind Russia for over half of the space race, they leaped ahead and won!

Joy filled the hearts of Americans as radio transmissions reported, "The Eagle has landed." Incredibly, in July of 1869 Professor Oberth's grandfather, Dr. Friedrich Krasser, said to his friends at a party, "You may believe it or not, but I am convinced that in a hundred years man will travel to the moon!" Twenty-five years later, Professor Oberth was born. Exactly one hundred years after Krasser's prophetic words the Apollo team landed on the moon.

**Astronaut Aldrin's first step onto the surface of the moon, July 1969.
(NASA-MSFC-6900937)**

The American Capture of Missile Technology

Through five manned missions of the Apollo program, six teams of astronauts explored the surface of our moon. Today, captured V-2 technology has evolved into propulsion systems that empower twelve-million pounds of thrust, and has expanded our influence out to the far reaches of our solar system. The Hubble Space Telescope gives us unprecedented views of deep space. Global Positioning Satellite Systems (GPS Systems) offer absolute location and are therefore used in air, land, and sea navigation; they are used to guide smart bombs, to locate and monitor convicts, and to help solve crimes. General Schwarzkopf praised satellite systems for being the backbone of his success with Operation Desert Storm. Presently, GPS systems continue to be an invaluable tool in the War on Terror.

Moreover, captured missile technology led to America achieving superiority at sea through the creation of Fleet Ballistic Missile Submarines (armed with long-range strategic missiles) more technologically advanced than any in the world. The CNN Interactive Website states, "The competitive nature of the cold war quickly fueled the creation of intercontinental ballistic missiles, lunar landers and space stations, and eventually gave birth to important inventions like the computer. In twenty-five short years, the world evolved from primitive rockets to manned missions to the moon."

John Galione was stunned that the result of his discovery of Camp Dora and the ensuing capture of missile technology led to the Space Race, and as he watched the United States expand upon captured technology he was astounded by the enormity of its influence on the world. Nevertheless, make no mistake: Galione was tortured his entire life after having witnessed the horrific murders, the pain, and the cruelty that the Nazis inflicted upon the prisoners of Dora-Nordhausen for the sake of these rockets. He spent his remaining years trying to make sense of their suffering.

Likewise, the moon landing caused pain for Mittelbau survivors who wondered why justice had not been served. When Neal Armstrong uttered the famous words, "That's one small step for man, one giant leap for mankind" those who survived the hell of Camp Dora remembered their fellow inmates who had died making von Braun's first rockets. "Everything that is now in space had its origins here at Camp Dora, not in America or Russia," said French Dora survivor, Rene Steenbeke. "This is where a new science started, but it is also where science and death met."

Very few of the leaders behind the nightmare of Camp Dora were punished for their war crimes. By the end of the war, Himmler, Hitler, and Goebbels had killed themselves. Rumors circulated that Kammler escaped capture by having his aides shoot him dead in Prague. Albert Speer served at Spandau prison. Arthur Rudolph was deported from America and sent back to Germany for his war crimes after being pursued by the Office of Special Investigations in Washington. As a result of the 1947 Dora-Mittelbau trial, SS Camp Leader Hans Karl Moeser was the only man sentenced to "death by hanging." But aside from eighteen defendants who received sentences ranging from five years to life imprisonment, scores of men behind the V-2 missile slave labor operation went on to become American heroes.

In fact, their transfer to the United States led to opening a huge new industry in America. They became executives of the government companies that manufactured parts for American spaceships and weapons of International Defense. Peenemünde's V-2 flight test director, Kurt Debus, became the first director of the Kennedy Space Center in Florida. Peenemünde's base commander, Major General Dornberger, became vice-president of Bell Aero Systems in New York. Peenemünde's technical director and developer of rocket motor control vanes, Martin Shilling, became president of Raytheon. Von Braun and his team became the nucleus of ABMA and NASA.

In early 1977, President Gerald Ford awarded Wernher von Braun the National Medal of Science. Survivors were outraged when after the moon landing and the placement of satellites von Braun and his team became American heroes, living lavishly and receiving honor and rewards instead of penalty for their part in slave labor. Although von Braun fans say that he and the team who developed V-2 technology did not create the political conditions that made Camp Dora, a memo was found proving that von Braun had actively sought out using slave laborers from Buchenwald to make missiles at Dora. Survivors say he saw their suffering and demonstrated indifference.

The survivors who suffered the nightmare of Dora remembered the countless thousands of people who died making their rockets. Heartbroken and angry, Mittelbau Dora survivors asked, "How important was it to get to the moon? Was it worth the tens of thousands who suffered unspeakable tortures and died in the utmost despair? After all the torment we suffered in the name of this rocket, why would fate, or even God, allow von Braun and his team of Nazi scientists to come to the United States and become heroes!?"

Chapter 6

Decoding History:
God and the Holocaust

In an attempt to find something positive in the most painful chapter of their lives, Holocaust survivors searched written histories, hoping to find evidence of God's involvement in their rescue and His compassion toward those who suffered in the camps. But, after years of study some said, "There is no God." Others concluded, "If there is a God, He doesn't care about people." A Jewish woman who survived the horror of Buchenwald hollered in anguish on national television, asking, "If God loved us so much, then why didn't he save us before the evacuation of the camps? Why did He wait until most of us were *dead!?*"

When Galione realized survivors were heartbroken, thinking God had forgotten them, he mourned that he had kept secret the one war story that contained the evidence they searched for. Then, history was further obscured as it was written to impress the Russians, leaving out the key historical events that play an important part in establishing accurate post-war conclusions. As the soldier who initiated the search for prisoners before the infantry knew of Dora, who searched for the camp, found the camp, inspected the camp, sought for and acquired help to break into the camp, led bands of liberators to the camp and filmed the camp and the atrocities there, Galione possessed a wealth of historical knowledge that gave him the advantage of drawing important conclusions from a more complete knowledge of history than the one that was written.

Using the same engineering mind that enabled him after the war to invent the pollution system that kept five 3M Manufacturing plants from closing, Galione spent a lifetime working to decode the complete history of all he had experienced in his life, in the war, and in Camp Dora. He spent years deciphering the horrors, counting the miracles, and exploring their deeper meaning. In the end, Galione began to see within his story the appearance of the fingerprints of God.

HAPPENSTANCE OR INTERVENTION

As a result of Galione's story being kept under wraps, history states that Camp Dora was discovered "as the troops advanced to Nordhausen." Today, survivors and liberators both agree that Camp Dora was not on the beaten path of the American Army. Galione experienced firsthand that Camp Dora was not found by mere happenstance. He stated that he experienced a Strong Force that urged him to "follow the trains", that pushed him to keep him from turning around and aborting the mission, that strengthened him when he was too exhausted to keep walking. After years of pondering his experience, he drew an important conclusion that he believed would mean a great deal to the survivors who sought to find within the written histories the evidence of God's involvement in their rescue:

> For years I tried to figure out who pushed me by the trains and led me to the camp. I figured it had to be one of three things: God, an angel, or the spirits of the dead people that I found in the train car. Then one day I realized that when the Force pushed me to stop me from turning around, I had not yet actually turned around. I was only *thinking* of turning around. That's when I realized that it had to be God Himself who was behind it, because only God could have known what I was thinking; only God knows our thoughts.

Galione concluded he was sent on a "detour" to follow the train tracks because the American troops were going to *miss* the hidden Camp Dora as they advanced to Berlin. When he radioed Combat B of the Third Armored Division to give them directions to Camp Dora, he realized they had *missed* the camp. "They never saw it," he said. "One group had passed the camp, and the other group wasn't in an area where they would have advanced upon the camp."

As a result of their location, when Private Galione gave them directions to Camp Dora he instructed them to "divert" to the Nordhausen area where they would find "something unique." In a letter dated August 15, 2002, Timberwolf veteran, Rip Rice, of the 329th Engineers H & S Company remembers the day the call came in: "As I recall, we were not supposed to go to Nordhausen. We were on our way to Halle, but on the way we were ordered to 'divert' to the Nordhausen area for 'something unique.'" In a subsequent letter, Rice states that the "hidden location of the Nordhausen missile factory was clearly out of the path of the Timberwolves toward Halle, Leipzig and Berlin." In a letter dated August 9, 2005, Dora survivor, George Benedict, agrees: "I doubt that any Army would rush to Nordhausen," he wrote. "Even today, after Germany is reunited, Nordhausen is 'out of the way.' It is not on the 'main path.'"

While considering the location of the troops in relation to the camp, Private Galione realized that when he left his encampment to follow the trains a crucial moment in time had taken place in history for the United States of America and for the prisoners of Dora and related camps. "If I hadn't left when I did," said Galione, "the Russians would have gotten it all and the prisoners would have all died."

According to a recent History Channel documentary on spy technology, if the Russians had gotten all of Dora's missile technology behind America's back, the United States could have suffered a nuclear war—and New York might have been their first target! After their transfer to America, German scientists revealed they had been developing a "Vengeance Missile" to hit New York. However, Galione's persistence in following the trains secured the perfect timing that enabled the Americans to beat the Russians by mere hours to confiscating *all* the secret weapons and top German scientists.

As a result, the sharing of German missile and satellite technology between the United States and Russia caused a cold war competition so neck-in-neck that it procured world peace through the threat of mutual destruction. President Eisenhower recognized this outcome. After the first twelve years of the cold war he stated that the knowledge gained by both Russia and America was a "deterrent to war" because "any attack on us and our Allies would result, regardless of damage to us, in their own national destruction."

Through Satellite technology, one nation couldn't move without the other seeing. Through missile technology, one nation couldn't strike without the other striking back. The Department of Defense labeled this unique situation "Mutual Assured Destruction" (M.A.D.). In fact, having the Germans developing missiles in America parallel to the Russians was so important to National Security that any part German engineers played in Dora's slave labor was hushed so they would not have to leave America to face trial.

Galione was traumatized his entire life by the horrors he saw in both Dora and Nordhausen. He grieved that the victims of these camps suffered horribly and never received full justice. Yet, he realized that the United States couldn't make a find like the world's first ballistic missile and simply walk away. As the Russians moved forward with military programs designed to kill Americans, justice was sacrificed to ensure International Security. Having the United States and Russia share German technology was the only way to protect America and her Allies from nuclear war with Russia. At the very least, the sharing of power kept the United States from enduring a nuclear threat that may have been used as leverage to take from Americans the freedom enjoyed today.

During the cold war, John Galione saw hidden wisdom in the fact that the Germans spent a lifetime developing and perfecting the ballistic missile, and the Russians spent months calculating its capture, yet it was God who chose the nation to be responsible for that power when He sent an American soldier to follow the trains. Galione was a humble man who never considered himself a hero, yet he recognized that only the wisdom of God could have achieved world peace. Galione concluded had he not taken the detour to Camp Dora, U.S. satellites and missiles would today be Russian satellites and missiles, and Americans would be speaking Russian. A History Channel documentary on Mittelbau Dora agreed by stating: "If Camp Dora hadn't been found when it was, the footprint on the moon would have been Russian."

In light of the complete history, Galione drew the conclusion that God, having invaluable foresight, allowed (but not preferred) the coming of top German scientists to America—not to reward them for their crimes, but to use them to prevent further war and suffering that would have come about if Stalin had gotten it all. In other words, He made them rectify the dangerous situation their missiles had caused between the nations in order to prevent a nuclear holocaust. His ingenious plan for a cold war standoff rendered the missiles mute for decades and the United States remains a free country in peace with Russia to this day.

From his red toy rocket wagon to high-tech missiles and the placement of satellites, to the *Saturn* rockets that thrust the first men to the moon, clearly Wernher von Braun was determined to make a nation a superpower. Private Galione's destiny was to ensure that nation was the United States of America. Why would God influence the events that made America the greatest nation on earth?

Today fascist regimes are working to acquire and develop nuclear weapons in order to remove freedom—and Israel—from the face of the earth. Russia is helping those regimes to develop the weapons that can achieve these goals. Had the Russians made an exclusive capture of German missile technology in 1945, both the United States and Israel might have been conquered long ago. Conversely, the United States shared captured technology with Israel, which helped them to triumph during the Six-Day-War. Israel is a small country surrounded by enemies who are constantly plotting to destroy it. Captured V-2 technology made America the superpower of the world. America has been Israel's greatest Ally and place of refuge for decades. As Private Galione followed the trains to Camp Dora he sensed the importance of his mission, yet he had no idea his war effort would help to ensure the preservation of the United States and her Allies, including Israel. Even so, it remains to be seen how Divine Wisdom can procure peace today with a new and irrational enemy who welcomes, and even provokes, the threat of mutual destruction.

SAVING THE WEAKEST FIRST

When Galione instructed the Third Armored Division to get to Dora first in order to protect the Timberwolves from ambush, Dora was so hidden they got lost and found Nordhausen Death Camp on the way to Dora by accident. Galione believed this key historical event of the troops getting lost on the way to Camp Dora and ending up at Camp Nordhausen was virtually left out of written history because the troops thought they had made two mistakes better left unsaid: first passing or missing the camp, then getting lost after being called to the camp to protect an attachment from a potential ambush. Yet, Galione believed that the troops who got lost on the way to Camp Dora and ended up at Nordhausen Death Camp had not made a mistake at all, but had taken part in the miracle of Divine Intervention. Galione concluded the mishap occurred because God was trying to save the weakest first.

"It was God's wisdom that sent me, a single soldier, to Camp Dora where there would be only one German guard to contend with," said Galione, "but He sent the largest armored division of the United States Army to Nordhausen" where the most emaciated Jews who had been through the ranks of camps lay dying on straw mixed with excrement, amidst a swarm of cruel guards in the process of killing them all. That's when the 555th AAA came crashing through the barbed wire fencing and found a pile of very small children still burning. "They knew from the size of the bones," said Galione, "that they were babies and toddlers under five-years-old."

Private Galione's heroic war effort reached beyond the rescue of Dora prisoners. When he asked for permission to search for prisoners on April 4, the military objective was to kill Germans and get to Hitler—*not find camps*. According to Mittelbau-Dora historian, Gretchen Schafft, who authored the book *From Racism to Genocide*, "even after Camp Ohrdruf was discovered (the first camp found by the Americans) the American soldiers were not ordered to search for camps. They were told to 'Do what you're there to do: Fight the war. Let Germany clean up her own mess.'" But after Galione's scouting mission exposed the world's first ballistic missile being assembled in a secret labyrinth by slave laborers, the Pentagon ordered the search for all remaining camps and weapons. In brief, Private Galione's discovery of the ballistic missile camp not only caused the troops to "divert" back to the camps, but also changed the military objective to search for all remaining camps, saving the remnant of prisoners in the German camps.

MIRACLE AT THE MARK RIVER

As Galione processed the deeper meaning of the miracles that occurred in the midst of evil and war, he expounded on the Mark River Crossing. Private Galione, Leonard Puryear, and a third man were the only three men who survived the crossing of the Mark River from their entire group. The rest were killed. Then, Puryear was made sergeant when his sergeant became a casualty. At the time, Puryear's comrades thought he was "too quiet and shy" to become sergeant. But after a lifetime of pondering the events, Galione realized that God had spared the two of them at the Mark River *and* had made Puryear sergeant all in an effort to ensure the rescue of the remnant of prisoners at Dora and related camps.

> When we were the only three men who survived the Mark River from our group, we had a strong feeling when we were resting in the barn that there was a divine reason we had been spared. I don't know what the reason was for the third man who survived, but I know why Len and I were saved. I was supposed to find the camp and the sarge was supposed to agree to go in and rescue. God had planned it all beforehand. You see, any other sergeant during *that* time of the war would have said *no* to going in and rescuing, but he said, *yes!* He did the right thing and I was proud of him for that.

THE SURVIVORS' DESPERATE PRAYER

After reading Private Galione's war account, Dora survivor Yves Beón telephoned Galione's daughter Mary and said, "Your father was the soldier we prayed for. Read my book!" In his book, *Planet Dora*, Yves stated that the prisoners prayed for a soldier that would hear their cries, who would be injected with madness that will make him plunge forward enough to free us; a soldier who would charge on in spite of his wounds, who would push a broken vehicle, keep on without stopping, and sleep only after finding the prisoners.

As in Yves' prayer, Private Galione caused two advances in Germany (Aachen and the Roer River) that enabled the troops to advance. Later, he sensed the cries of suffering prisoners from within his soul and was so driven to find them that he plunged forward and walked with a nagging leg wound through Nazi territory from the Lippstadt area to Thuringia. After five days of walking, he slept only *after* finding the prisoners at Dora's main gate. He then walked again to seek help, repaired a broken jeep, and returned the next morning with soldiers to help him break into the camp. The slogan for the 104th Infantry Division states: "Nothing in hell can stop the Timberwolves." Galione did not stop until he had ensured that hundreds of service members from various troops were on their way to rescue the remaining prisoners of Mittelbau Dora Concentration Camp.

THE FORTIFICATION OF HATE

After a lifetime of mulling over the finer details of the complete history, Galione drew a final conclusion about God and the holocaust: "I'm convinced," said Galione solemnly with tears welling. "He would have saved them all if He could, but the forces in Germany were great."

Galione's statement is not to be misconstrued. He is not saying that Nazi forces were more powerful than God. He is referring to the fact that "*people*" are God's hands and feet. Hate had been allowed to fester and grow in Germany for so long that it rose to an evil force of monstrous proportions. As a result, fear immobilized people's goodness and courage. How could He save them all when there were too few willing to take the risks necessary to save them? One of the most important lessons drawn from Galione's conclusions is that in order to prevent another holocaust, the nations should never allow hate to prosper and grow.

Private Galione never knew the origin of the foul odor that prompted him to search for prisoners; yet, he was willing to walk a hundred miles alone through enemy territory in order to find them, and his actions changed world history. Likewise, Sergeant Puryear agreed to the rescue even though he knew the troops were battle-weary. Although Galione and his sergeant were not included in written history for more than half a century, their actions live on in the grandchildren of the people they saved and in the freedom Americans enjoy today.

Chapter 7

A Message Emerged

After years of study and coming up empty as to why God would allow the senseless murder of millions of innocent people in the camps, holocaust survivors asked God one final heart-rending question: "Did you at least care about our suffering?" After a lifetime of mulling over the comprehensive history, John Galione made the astonishing discovery that the answer to their question had been written within the story of his life and had emerged as an astounding holocaust memorial. Suddenly, maintaining secrecy became insignificant next to the meaning his story would bring to the survivors and to their loved ones. John Galione may have returned home from war unknown and undecorated, but as he reached the end of his remarkable life story he said to Mary, "You know how I never received any sort of military reward for what I had done to save the people? Well, God would not let me go undecorated after the war."

"What do you mean," asked Mary. "How does an Invisible Force pin a medal on you? How does God decorate a soldier?"

Galione reveals the astonishing conclusion:

> The first baby I had that was born after the war was born dead. Her whole body was completely blue from head to toe from lack of oxygen. The doctor said she had been without oxygen for too long because of the placenta. There was no hope. She weighed only four or five pounds. She looked so pitiful just lying there so quiet in his arms. The doctor was about to turn around and take her to the morgue when I said, "Wait!" I don't know what it was, but I just had a feeling.

"What do you want me to do?" the doctor asked. "There is no hope. She is gone."

"We can't just call it quits without giving it a try to revive her," I said.

The doctor said she had been dead too long and there was no hope, but he agreed to give it a try, just to make me feel better. He worked on her and in about twelve minutes the color started to come back into her body. In twenty minutes she started to breathe and was revived. It was a miracle! She was born dead and came back to life—*and it all happened on the anniversary date of the liberation of the people I saved!*

But the blessing didn't stop there. To add to this blessing, the baby who was born dead grew up, and twenty years later her firstborn daughter was born on that same day. *On the liberation date of the camp!* Then, about another twenty years later your firstborn son, Daniel, was born the day before, during the liberation dates of Dora and Nordhausen. Then, his brother Michael was born exactly one year later in April. Everything that happened to me after the war was as though God was saying "Thanks!" repeatedly. Even you were born on Thanksgiving Day (Jewish calendar). I had you in my arms on that day.

With all these births falling on the liberation dates of the camp every twenty years, as though God had made a memorial; and with one of them being brought back from the dead *on that day*, I felt like God was trying to tell me something. You know how no one ever knew what I did to save the people, and how I never received recognition or military decoration? I felt like God was trying to tell me that *He* knew what I did to save the people and He was *happy*. He was trying to say that I had done *well* and he was *thankful*. And when my baby came back from the dead: *That* was better than any military reward I could have ever received!

Then, when your sister was in a coma from the car accident and the doctor told me she was going to die, I prayed to God my most sincere and fervent prayer. I said, "Dear God, the doctor tells me that my daughter is going to die, but this is the baby you gave back to me in return for saving the people. I find it very hard to believe that you would give her back to me for this purpose so many years ago only to take her from me now. But if it is your will to take her, Dear God, then so be it." It was right after I prayed that prayer that she came out of the coma and the doctor informed me that her prognosis went from *death* to *life!*

But there was another message God was trying to send me in all those miracles. When my baby was born dead and brought back to life on the anniversary date of the liberation of the camp I thought to myself, "God gave me back my baby in return for saving the people." Then, when her baby was born twenty years later on that same day, I thought, "God has made a memorial to remind me that he saved my baby in return for what I did to save the people." But when Daniel was born another twenty years later on the liberation date, I felt there was something more that He was trying to tell me, but I didn't yet know what it was. Then, when Michael was born exactly one year later in April, instead of twenty years later like the others, I realized what God had been trying to tell me.

The reason Michael was born one year later instead of twenty years later like the others is because I don't have another twenty years left to live and God wants me to tell my story now, during this generation. Mary, I want you to write my story. When you write the story, don't just tell them *how* I found them, but I want you to tell them of all the miracles that happened to me before and after the war. You see, if the survivors could know how God blessed me after the war in return for what I did to save the people, then they will know that God was *happy* they were saved, and if He was so *happy* they were saved that He gave me babies born on the liberation date of the camps every twenty years, and one of those babies was born dead and brought back to life on that day, then they'll know He cared about them. They'll know He loved them and never wanted them to suffer and die like that. But then I wondered, "Why was God so happy when I only saved the few, but so many thousands had died?"

AN ASTONISHING MESSAGE EMERGED

As Galione processed the comprehensive history, a correlation emerged that contained the answer to his question. Galione recognized that the shower of emotion and blessing he received from God after the war resembled the shower of emotion he received from his mother upon returning to her alive from the frozen river.

> She grabbed me *hard* and pulled me into her. She was holding me tight, crying out my name, *"Johnny! Johnny!"* and kissing me all over, thanking God over and over again for bringing me back to her. My mother had lost so many children that she couldn't bear the thought of losing one more. She was so grateful that I didn't die, that I came back to her.

Suddenly, Galione realized that his mother had not been crying out *his* name, but the name of the brother he was named after, the son she loved who had died. That's when he realized that in the same way that his mother embraced him with joy for surviving the river, while simultaneously crying out the name of the son who had died, so God embraced Galione with joy for saving the few, while crying out the names of the millions who suffered and died. Like Elisabetta, God had grieved the loss of so many of His children in the holocaust that He couldn't bear the thought of one more. He was so grateful that the remnant was saved.

THE SIGNIFICANCE OF THE RIVER INCIDENT

Galione wanted the survivors to know that God not only orchestrated their rescue through a series of miracles during the war, but He had been planning their rescue almost twenty years before the war when He saved Galione from drowning under the frozen ice of the Delaware River. Galione humbly expounds:

> For years I tried to remember how I got out from under the ice and onto the banks of the river. I tried to remember finding the hole and climbing across the ice, but I had no recollection of it. I tried to find who might have rescued me, but there was no one in sight for miles and there was only one set of footprints in the snow, and they were mine. Considering the importance of what came out of my life, what I ended up accomplishing in the war, I know now who it was that saved me: *God was not going to let me die until my purpose was fulfilled, and my purpose was to save the prisoners and cause the weapons to come here to America.* If I hadn't found the camp, the prisoners would have all died and the Germans would have been making the weapons for some other country—probably Russia, or maybe France or Britain because they were there too—but they wouldn't have come here, to this country. I'm sure of it.
>
> I want you to write my story, Mary. Not so that I become a hero, but because the prisoners were deprived of knowing the story behind their own rescue. This is important because they suffered so long and prayed so hard to be rescued; they thought God didn't care about them. They probably thought He had forgotten them. But if they knew of all the miracles that were unfolding as I searched for them, and the miracles that happened to me before and after the war (the river rescue and the blessing of the babies), they would know it was God who saved them. I was only the instrument He used to find them. I'm convinced: He

would have saved them all if He could, but the forces in Germany were great. (As stated in the previous chapter, Galione is not saying that Nazi forces were more powerful than God. He is saying that *"people"* are God's hands and feet. Hate had been allowed to fester and grow in Germany for so long that it rose to an evil force of monstrous proportions. As a result, fear immobilized people's goodness and courage.)

Tell them my story, Mary. It is the only good they'll have to think about when the dreadful name of Dora is mentioned. Someday when I die I want you to watch the film. I filmed a little bit of everything: the prisoners, the camp, the factory, and the tunnels. When I die and you see the film of how those people were treated, and when you see what was going on there in the tunnels, *then* you will know what your father has done.

I think about those people every year. Not a year goes by that I don't think about them. Your sister's birthday, Denise's birthday, and the birthdays of your sons, Daniel and Michael, are how I remember them. When I hear their birthdays are coming, I remember those poor people and the terrible shape they were in; and I wonder how many of them lived and if they were ever able to live normal lives, after all they had been through. Write my story, Mary. It will help them make peace with God as they reach the end of their lives.

In total, seven of Galione's offspring were born on these significant dates, including a grandchild born on Holocaust Remembrance Day and a great-granddaughter whose birth due-date was April 11, the day he broke into Camp Dora and called in the troops. John Galione concluded that God spent a lifetime building a memorial through these births, because He did not want this generation to pass without having the survivors and those who lost loved ones know that He was behind their rescue and that He loved them and never wanted them to suffer and die in the camps.

Iolé (later changed to Viola) and John Galione
upon his return from war in December of 1945

Late Summer or Fall of 1944: Galione and Harmanos at Camp Wheeler, Georgia. Left to right: Steve Harmanos, Tom Galanti, John Galione, and Norman Fenner.

John Galione (R) going house-to-house with two comrades.

Galione with the bazooka that destroyed with a single round the lead tank of a long line of tanks, enabling his unit's advance into the heart of Germany.

John Galione with daughter Mary in the summer of 1985.

Acknowledgements

Words cannot express my immense appreciation for the following people. The help and support of those mentioned enabled me to keep my promise to my father, whose incredible story will from this day forward be included in written history.

Dora survivors, their families, Timberwolf sergeants, Mittelbau Dora Board of Directors and others who provided me with translations and official verification of my father's discovery: Michel Depierre, Josette Depierre, Sophie Depierre-Samuels, George Benedict, Charles and Joan Lang, Marie-Claire du Bois, Yves Beón, Alice Cordisco, Lorraine Harmanos-Heinrich, Timberwolf Sergeants Leonard Puryear, John Youngs, and Gerald De Veaux (415th regiment, company B), Leo Thoennes (555th).

Research and other Support: Jeanne, Adrie, Bart and Teun Oostvogels, Robert Caggiano, Jean-Claude Augst, Alan S. Batens, Leo Thoennes, Milt and Rae Gilbert, Edmundo Velazquez, Jean Michel, Abraham Biderman, Michael Neufeld, Tracy Dungan, Paul Griegorieff, Reidsville Library, Denise Kolber, Harold and Carol Mitchener, Michael Tillman, Cress Warner, the two men from British Guiana, Rabbis Shimon Apisdorf, Raphael Butler, and Barry Mase; Rachel Laufer, and the Afikim Foundation; Rabbi Maurice E. Novoseller.

Photos: Fred Deaton, Raymond T. Downward of NASA's Marshall Space Flight Center; Holly Reed, Shanna Smith of NARA; Clause Martel, Kaylene Hughes of AMCOM at Redstone Arsenal; Barry Spink, Jim Tynan of the Civil Air Patrol; Peter Woodcock, Norman Yates, RAF Association; the Buchenwald-Dora Memorials; Nancy Hartman and the United States Holocaust Memorial Museum.

Family Support: My husband John and our three wonderful children, Veronica, Daniel, and Michael.

Bibliography

Ayer, Eleanor H. *The Survivors.*
California: Lucent Books, 1998.

Bachrach, Deborah. *The Resistance.*
California: Lucent Books, 1998.

Beón, Yves. *Planet Dora: A Memoir of the Holocaust and the Birth of the Space Age.* Colorado: Westview Press, 1997.

Biderman, Abraham H. *The World of My Past.*
Australia: Random House, 1995.

Lace, William. *Death Camps.*
California: Lucent Books, 1998.

Michel, Jean. *Dora: The Nazi Concentration Camp Where Modern Space Technology was Born and 30,000 Prisoners Died.* Translated from French by Jennifer Kidd.
New York: Holt, Rinehart and Winston, 1979.

Neufeld, Michael J. *The Rocket and the Reich: Peenemünde and the Coming of the Ballistic Missile Era.* Massachusetts: Harvard University Press, 1995.
The Free Press, a division of Simon & Shuster, Inc., 1995.

Rice, Earle Jr. *Nazi War Criminals.*
California: Lucent Books, 1998.

Rice, Earle Jr. *The Final Solution.*
California: Lucent Books, 1998.

Speer, Albert. *Inside the Third Reich.*
Translated from German by Richard and Clara Winston.
New York: Macmillan Co., 1970.

Speer, Albert. *Infiltration: How Heinrich Himmler Schemed to Build an SS Industrial Empire.* New York: Macmillan Co., 1981.

von Braun, Wernher, Frederick I. Ordway III. *The Rockets' Red Glare.*
New York: Anchor Press Doubleday, 1976.

Walters, Helen B. *Wernher von Braun: Rocket Engineer.*
New York: Macmillian Company, 1964.

Grigorieff, Paul. *The Mittelwerk/Mittelbau/Camp Dora*
V2Rocket.com, T. Dungan

The Chicago Manual of Style: *15th edition.* Edited by Alice Bennett.
Chicago and London: The University of Chicago Press, 2003.

End Notes to Chapter 4

1. Robert Goddard, an American, was the first to design and launch a liquid-fueled rocket on March 16, 1926, but he kept his work secret as the Germans gained publicity.
2. Nelson C. Eaton of the 929 HQ Field Artillery Battalion wrote in his account: "It wasn't but a few minutes until we received word from one of our 'infantry companies' that they had found something big but couldn't make it out, nor could they get in." (Eaton's account is posted on the Official 104th Infantry Division website.)
3. Nelson C. Eaton of the 929 HQ Field Artillery Battalion wrote in his account: "The Infantry Battalion Commander said he would go down and have a look, and asked me to go along. We arrived at this large wire and board fenced-in area with a strong lock on the gate."
4. Nelson Eaton of the 929 HQ Field Artillery Battalion wrote in his account: "We soon had the lock broken, and what we found inside was beyond explanation."
5. October 7, 1998 Colonel William L. Howard wrote in his account that "Intelligence" had alerted the Third Armored Division to "expect something a little unusual in the Nordhausen area." The "Intelligence" he is speaking of is Private John Galione. On April 11, 1945, Galione radioed Combat Command Boudinot (Taskforce Lovelady and Taskforce Wellborn) of the Third Armored Division, along with other 104th Infantry Division attachments to give them directions to Camp Dora. Sergeant Puryear notified Colonel Taggart and the medical teams.
6. Captain William Warmington of the 555th AAA, the first to drive over the barbed-wire fencing of Camp Nordhausen, wrote in his memoir: "On April 12 the division . . . proved to be the best defense for the division against the frequent 'ambushing' of convoys." (Handwritten account: Courtesy of William's son, John Warmington.)
7. On page 329 and 330 of the Timberwolf Tracks History Book Sergeant Ragene Farris of the 329th Medical Battalion states: "Our S-2, Captain Johnson, brought the news that we were needed to evacuate

patients from a concentration camp in one of the large factory areas of the city. Colonel Taggart called into action early 12 April, the litter bearers and medical technicians as well as any other men available from duties with our own wounded. In a caravan of trucks we rushed into a job which proved fantastic and unbelievable to an American; a job distasteful and sobering; one created by the fanatical inhuman Nazi machine. We found out the full meaning of the words, Concentration Camp."

8 Timberwolf Rip Rice of the 329th Engineers H & S Company wrote in a letter dated August 15, 2002: "As I recall, we were not supposed to go to Nordhausen. We were on our way to Halle; but along the way, we were ordered to 'divert' to the Nordhausen area for 'something unique'."

9 Exhausted and war weary, Private Galione forgot to tell the Third Armored Division to look for a curve in the road when trying to find Camp Dora, as the hidden location of Camp Dora made it impossible to see the camp when looking down the main road.

10 On page 329 and 330 of Timberwolf Tracks it states: "The 414th, which had been attached to the [Third] Armored since 22 March, was to revert to the 104th midnight 11 April." Since Galione had found the camp, he was given the task of leading the 414th (Taskforce Kelleher) to Camp Dora in the dark early morning as April 11 turned to April 12.

11 With Galione being told not to tell anyone he had discovered Camp Dora, he feared another infantry division might be wrongly credited for the discovery. Therefore, Galione was glad other Timberwolves (such as the 555th AAA) had found the Mittelbau Dora sub-camp, Nordhausen Death Camp, on the way to Mittelbau Dora. "If our division had not received the credit for the liberation as a result of my being silenced, then I would have come forward and told my story, that it was I who found the camp."

12 Although pork is forbidden in Jewish law the most observant rabbis say that a commandment can be broken if doing so saves a life. In this case, about 1,200 lives were saved. In regard to the pork soup, orthodox rabbis have said to Galione's daughter, "Your father did the right thing."

Mittelbau Dora Memorial

Director: Dr. Jens-Christian Wagner

Kohnsteinweg 20, 99734, Nordhausen, Germany

Bio and Website

Mary Nahas is Private Galione's daughter. She is a veterans' advocate and holocaust educator who speaks in universities and at military events. Mary is also an avid researcher who has written more than sixty articles for various newspapers. Her next book tells of an enthralling, ancient history that reveals the spiritual root of anti-Semitism.

The Heroic Journey of Private Galione is available at

www.amazon.com

Visit www.JohnGalione.com for more information

Printed in Great Britain
by Amazon.co.uk, Ltd.,
Marston Gate.